THE FAITH WE HAVE NOT KEPT

By
SENATOR STROM THURMOND

VIEWPOINT BOOKS
San Diego, California 92109
A Division of Loeffler & Co., Inc.

THE FAITH WE HAVE NOT KEPT

Second Printing, September 1968

ABOUT THE AUTHOR

U.S. Senator Strom Thurmond, a lawyer and farmer, was born and reared in Edgefield County, South Carolina, where he made his home until he became Governor of South Carolina in 1947. During his first year as Governor, he was married in the Governor's mansion to Jean Crouch of Elko. Upon leaving the Governor's office in 1951, the Thurmonds moved to Aiken, S.C., where he engaged in an active practice of law until December 24, 1954. At that time he began his service in the United States Senate, and has been re-elected to successive terms. Mrs. Thurmond passed away in 1960 as a result of a malignant brain tumor.

U.S. Senate

Senator Thurmond is noted in the Senate for his independence, his adherence to strong constitutional principles, his consistent record of voting for economy in government, his strong support of military preparedness, and his articulate advocacy of a winning policy in Vietnam. He serves on the following important committees and subcommittees:

Major Committee Posts

Armed Services
Judiciary
Appropriations (Defense)
Republican Campaign

Armed Services Subcommittees

Preparedness Investigating
Military Construction
Central Intelligence Agency
NATO Status of Forces
Code of Uniform Military Justice

Judiciary Subcommittees

Internal Security
Juvenile Delinquency
Criminal Laws & Procedures
Constitutional Amendments
Immigration & Naturalization
Constitutional Rights
Administrative Practice & Procedure

Civilian Service and Civilian Awards

Senator Thurmond had a variety of experience in public service prior to his election to the U.S. Senate. A graduate of Clemson College (now Clemson University), he has farmed, worked in a textile mill, taught school and coached athletics, served as County Superintendent of Education, practiced law, and served in all three branches of the State government—as State Senator, Circuit Judge, and Governor of South Carolina (1947-1951). His national awards include the Order of Lafayette Freedom Award; Young Americans for Freedom Government Award; Military Order of World Wars Distinguished Service Award; National Society, Sons of the American Revolution for outstanding services; National Society, Daughters of the American Revolution, for Notable Patrotic Service; and Americans for Constitutional Action Distinguished Service Award. Among his other awards are American Legion, Department of South Carolina, Distinguished Public Service Award; Sertoma International Service to Mankind Award; Clemson College Alumni Distinguished Service Award; and five honorary degrees. Thurmond Hall at Winthrop College, streets in several cities, and Strom Thurmond High School in his native county of Edgefield, were named in his honor. A biography of his life, *Rebel Senator: Strom Thurmond of South Carolina*, was published in 1966 by the Devin-Adair Company, New York.

Military Service and Military Awards

Senator Thurmond is an ROTC graduate. He served in World War II in both the European and Pacific Theaters. For his performance in military service, active and reserve, he has been awarded five battle stars and 17 decorations, medals, and awards, including the Legion of Merit, Bronze Star for Valor in Combat, Army Commendation, Purple Heart, Belgian Order of the Crown, and French Croix de Guerre. In the Army Reserve, he attained the rank of Major General. He has served as National President of the Reserve Officers Association of the United States and of The Military Government Association.

History Making Achievements

In World War II, Senator Thurmond voluntarily gave up the security of a circuit judgeship to serve his country in uniform. On D-Day, he volunteered to be dropped behind German lines in Normandy with the 82nd Airborne Division.

In 1948, then Governor of South Carolina, he was the States Rights Democratic candidate for President, carrying four States and winning 39 electoral votes (largest of any third party candidate since Teddy Roosevelt and second largest ever).

In 1954, he was elected to the U.S. Senate in a write-in campaign, being the first person ever elected to a major office in the U.S. by this method.

In 1956, he kept his campaign promise and resigned as U.S. Senator, in order to let the people choose in a free election. He was re-elected without opposition.

In 1957, he delivered the longest speech ever made in the U.S. Senate (24 hours, 18 minutes). It was in defense of jury trials.

In 1961, he coined the phrase "no-win" foreign policy, and warned that such a policy is based on the fallacious notion that Communist leaders are softening.

In 1961, he single-handedly launched an investigation into Defense Secretary McNamara's muzzling of the military and the perils of the Secretary's de-emphasis of military preparedness.

In January, 1962, he warned that Soviet missiles were in Cuba, almost a year before the Kennedy Administration took action.

In 1963, he caused the first secret Senate session since World War II to debate military preparedness and to warn that Russia had initiated deployment of an anti-ballistic missile system. Since 1957, he has consistently urged the development of an effective U.S. ABM defense.

On September 16, 1964, he switched from the Democratic to the Republican Party, in order to fight more effectively for the cause of freedom.

In 1966, he was the first person in the history of South Carolina to be elected by the people to the U.S. Senate on a Republican ticket.

DEDICATION

This book is fondly dedicated to the memory of my parents, John William Thurmond and Eleanor Gertrude Strom Thurmond, whose living example of good citizenship and love of God and country inspired me to a life of public service.

"The way to have good and safe government is not to trust it all to one; but to divide it among the many, distributing to every one exactly the functions he is competent to do.

"Let the national government be entrusted with the defense of the nation, and its foreign and federal regulations; the state government with the civil rights, laws, police and administration of what concerns the state generally; the counties with the local concerns of the counties and each ward direct the interests within itself.

"It is by dividing and subdividing these republics, from the great national one down through all its subordinations, until it ends in the administration of every man's farm and affairs by himself; . . . that all will be done for the best.

"What has destroyed liberty and the rights of man in every government which has existed under the sun? The generalizing and concentrating all cares and powers into one body, no matter whether of the autocrats of Russia or France or of the aristocrats of a Venetian Senate."

THOMAS JEFFERSON

PREFACE

Now is the time for the individual citizen who loves this country to heed the warnings of history and take an active part in reclaiming our American heritage.

In this book, I have attempted to describe the major issues that confront us, to trace their development, and to discuss remedial measures. It is impossible in a book of this length to go into great detail on every subject. I have tried, rather, to explain the basic problems by choosing examples which most clearly illustrate the malady. Simply because I have dwelt at length on a few illustrative examples does not mean that other examples could not have been chosen to dramatize the underlying principle as well. It is my belief that the value of a book on contemporary affairs comes out of the personal experience of the author. Those who are familiar with my career in the Senate will recognize most of the issues in this book as issues arising in areas to which I have devoted my public service.

Throughout the book, there is a constant theme that advocates return to constitutional principles of government, individual liberty, and free enterprise. There is also a warning against internal and external threats to our security, a call for economy in directing the affairs of the nation, and a mandate for the re-establishment of our sense of purpose in the world.

I have great hope for the future, and an abiding

faith that the American people will meet the challenge of the times and find the path to greater achievements. This will not be an easy task, but it can be done.

The first step is to recapture the spirit of our Founding Fathers and return to the principles of government they bequeathed us. Their priceless legacies, the Constitution and the American way of life, liberty, and the pursuit of happiness, cannot be realized unless we steadfastly keep faith with them. It is because we have not always kept that faith that we are so troubled today.

May, 1968.   STROM THURMOND

CONTENTS

Chapter I

DISORDER IN THE LAND

Here is America today.

In New York, a neighborhood political club invited a policeman over one evening to tell members how they could make the city's streets safe for walking. Quite a number of folks later said they missed the officer's talk because they had been afraid to walk to the meeting.

Is this freedom?

In Washington, a woman attacked by a man in a lonely self-service elevator screamed for help, punched wildly at the buttons, and managed to jam the elevator between floors. Police arrived quickly, but were unable to get into the elevator; while waiting for repairmen to arrive, they leaned into the shaft and began to advise the assailant on his Constitutional rights.

Is this freedom?

In Maryland one hot summer's night, a frenzied agitator from out of town with a whiplash tongue screamed this advice to the Negroes of Cambridge: "You built this town. Now go burn it down." They did; he left; and a few days later a Negro businessman, his hard-earned property in ruins, committed suicide.

Freedom for what?

1

Youngsters protest the war in Vietnam. After all, have not some prominent people offered to send blood to the enemy? The kids found out that burning draft cards make a pitiful flame, so they burn American flags instead. No one stops them. They do this in a place called Sheep Meadow.

Is there too much freedom, or too little freedom?

In Tennessee, an enterprising Internal Revenue Service agent, while reading a taxpayer's personal mail, conceived a new strategy: Finding a letter from "another woman," he showed it to the taxpayer's wife and pointed out that she could get revenge by informing on her erring husband's finances. The Internal Revenue Service said that it does not tolerate such conduct; however, the Service did continue to tolerate the agent. He got a "reprimand," and was left on the staff to think up new projects.

What's Happening

Go anywhere in America, and ask the people.

What is happening to us? Where are we heading?

In crowded cities, children are bused across town to strange schools and strange playmates in order to learn the current mathematics of the population mix. Although they are forced to play together, they are forbidden to pray together.

Is government doings things for us, or to us?

Is there less freedom now than before the Supreme Court began to worry more about the rights of criminals than of citizens?

Are riots as American as cherry pie?

Is patriotism as outmoded as apple pan dowdy?

The drift, and it is strong, is toward anarchy.

Disorder was not meant to be the harvest of liberty. In the grand vision, the fruits of freedom ought to be found in the ordinary citizen's daily life. He should arise in the morning free from interference from the state. He should be able to gather about him his family, educate his children as he pleases, walk undisturbed on the public streets. He ought to be allowed to speak what he will, worship as he pleases, and work where he wants and wherever they will have him. His property should be secure from arbitrary confiscation or attack; his person from arbitrary imprisonment; his rights from the hostile aggrandizement of his neighbor.

Such are the basic liberties of life. On the one hand, man needs protection from the offenses committed against him by his fellow man; and he needs protection from the state on the other. If the man who counts his blessings can count these among them, he is a free man.

The Constitution

After the Founding Fathers had struggled with the framing of the Constitution in Philadelphia in 1787, they had a pretty good idea of what they needed to do to establish freedom.

"We the People of the United States," they wrote, "in order to form a more perfect Union, establish Justice, insure domestic tranquility, provide for the common Defence, promote the general welfare, and secure the Blessings of Liberty to ourselves and our Posterity, do ordain and establish this CONSTITUTION for the United States of America."

Within every phrase, history would find a controversy.

What price a perfect Union?

If we are to establish Justice, whose Justice?

Can tranquility be guaranteed?

What must we defend ourselves against?

What is the general welfare, and can we plan to promote it?

What hope is at hand that our posterity will secure the blessings of liberty?

The progression of ideas leads inexorably to that last star-spangled question: *To secure the blessings of liberty.* Without that end in view, and attainable, the other goals are meaningless.

A perfect Union can be a perfect tyranny.

The pursuit of justice may leave behind the first and absolute principles.

Domestic tranquility may conceal a seething heart.

Defense of our sovereignty may be compromised by submission to supra-national organizations and arrangements.

The concept of "the general welfare" may be impoverished by confusing it with the standard of living.

The Constitution was not a blueprint for a "Great Society," nor a road map revealing the route to material plenty. It was intended to be a political instrument, fending off the tyranny of government on the one side, and the tyranny of the ungoverned multitude on the other. The Constitution contained no prescriptions for social organization. It said not one word about health, education, or scientific development. It held no brief for the economic well-being of the individual citizen, nor for the redistribution of the wealth.

What meaning does this document have for us

today? Is this truly a land of domestic tranquility, where the blessings of liberty are secure for ourselves and our posterity? Would our Founding Fathers think that we had kept the faith if they could return and observe our society?

Dissent and Distortion

No doubt they would be dismayed, first of all, to learn that the right of dissent and opposition, and the security of the rights of the individual have been distorted. These rights, so carefully preserved in the Constitution, are now used to sanction:

Flag burning and draft card burning.

Love of country being treated like a kind of social disease.

Boys and girls not having to study the history of our country, what it stands for, and the valiant efforts of our forefathers to preserve it.

Next they would see a society wracked by crime, violence and growing contempt for law. The FBI reports that crime is increasing at a rate of from ten to fifteen percent each year. The most recent FBI timetable shows that:

One murder occurred every 48 minutes.

One forcible rape occurred every 21 minutes.

One robbery occurred every 3 and 1/2 minutes.

One aggravated assault occurred every 2 minutes.

One burglary occurred every 23 seconds.

One serious larceny ($50 and over) occurred every 35 seconds.

One automobile theft occurred every 57 seconds.

There was a murder, forcible rape, or assault to kill every 2 minutes.

In one city, apartment dwellers watched a man being knifed to death on the street, but didn't call the police because "they didn't want to get involved."

The Founding Fathers knew about civil disorder firsthand. Shays' Rebellion in Massachusetts and the Whiskey Rebellion in Pennsylvania rocked the foundations of their early government. They understood group dissatisfactions and the urge to protest, and they knew how to deal with violence when it got out of hand. They ordered the Massachusetts State Militia to crush Shays' Rebellion and approved the stern suppression of the Whiskey Rebellion by George Washington's troops.

Riots Today

To them, today's rioting and mob violence would be unbelievable.

There were 101 major riots and scores of other incidents of violence in our cities during the three-year period 1965-1967. As a result 130 people were killed, 3,600 were injured, and property damage reached a total of $715 million.

It will take months to determine the extent of the damage resulting from the wave of riots that swept the country after the death of Martin Luther King. But statistics on arrests, fires and damage will not blot out the senseless savagery of the uncontrolled mobs. Both the assassination of King and the rioting that followed his death spring from the philosophy that each man is free to obey the laws which please him. As a result, there is more divisiveness, more fear and more resentment. Law-abiding Americans will long remember the spectacle of rioting in more than 80 cities, and the efforts of over 12,000 troops and city police trying to stem arson and looting in the nation's capital alone.

As a result of rising crime in the streets and mob violence the risk of an individual's being a crime victim has risen 48 percent since 1960. In 1966, there were 3,250,000 serious crimes reported to police, and it is well known that many crimes are never reported. The increase of youthful criminals means higher crime rates tomorrow—juvenile arrests for serious crime were 54 percent higher in 1966 than they were in 1960.

Violence today bespeaks a growing contempt for law. In the past, riots usually involved different groups of society—union members might have clashed with strike breakers, or whites with Negroes —but now the mob attacks policemen. Hooligans, crying "police brutality," assault law officers with bricks and fiery "molotov cocktails." In 1966, fifty-seven police officers were killed, and many more policemen, firemen and other public servants injured.

There are other signs of social disorder. Who can deny that our society is decaying, and that Americans are no longer the stable, God-fearing people who won our independence?

The breakdown of morality reveals promiscuity, illegitimate births and broken homes. In 1950, about one out of twenty-five children born in the United States was illegitimate. In 1960, this rose to one out of nineteen; in 1965 it was one out of fifteen. If this trend continues, by 1970 every tenth child in this country will be born out of wedlock.

The Founding Fathers charged the following generations to preserve the blessings of liberty for posterity. Like prudent heads of families, they admonished us not to waste our sustenance and to provide for our children's future. Have our bountiful resources been wisely used?

Here we must admit to fiscal irresponsibility. Our national budget is written in red ink. The heritage we have left our children is a soaring national debt. The debt reached a total of $352 billion in March 1968. Estimates for fiscal year 1968 show deficits from $18 billion to $30 billion. In other words, the expected shortage this year exceeds the total budget for operating the entire government in any year before World War II.

Deeper Tensions

More ominous still are the subsurface tensions among our people. Race is pitted against race in a way we have never seen before. Our nation's history is filled with accounts of sectional interests clashing with those of another region, of pressure groups which curry special favor, and of emotional propagandists who temporarily sweep reason and common sense by the wayside.

The new situation is different. The races have had differences before, but the divisions came about over political and economic questions. Now race *itself* is put forward as a sufficient cause of antagonism. Self-appointed experts have discouraged racial communities from developing wholesome and realistic goals for their members. The drive to remove separation between social communities has boomeranged. Segregated housing is being replaced by segregated hearts.

The President's Advisory Commission on Civil Disorders, which reported in March of 1968, profoundly misread the facts involved in the nation's civil disorders. The Commission's conclusions could not have been better calculated to foster a deepening division between the races in this country. The Commission was fighting fire with gasoline.

The attention of the news media focused primarily on a single sentence of the Commission's summary report; namely, "White racism is essentially responsible for the explosive mixture which has been accumulated in our cities since the end of World War II." Despite volumes of testimony taken for the purpose of establishing fact, the Commission presented only an assertive opinion.

It is plain that there are racists among both Negroes and whites, if the definition of "racism" includes the factor of hatred. It is an unfortunate fact of human nature that a man can choose of his own free will to hate another man. The truth seems to be that under normal circumstances such hatred is rare, but hatred is never justified.

The President's Commission oversimplified the mysteries of the human heart. Its report builds up stereotypes of hatred, and falsely accuses a whole people of vices they do not practice. The reaction of people to false accusations is predictable. The report has generated resentment, and undermined charitable attitudes.

Black racism is no more typical of human nature than white racism. The moderates find their good will flung back into their own faces. The report presented the spectacle of an official agency of the Federal Government supporting and giving credence to the inflammatory propaganda of militant, organized agitators.

The division extends to our cities, which now appear to be in runaway decline. At one time, the city was a place of rich associations, past and present. Men lived in cities because they were rooted there by ties of family, religion, history, culture, and the complex array of civilized contacts provided by a high density of population.

Our cities today are seats of crime and centers of deterioration. At first people fled to the suburbs in an attempt to recapture the peace and community that civilized life demands. They returned to the city only to work or to shop. Today the jobs and the stores have followed them into the developed countryside. The cities are dying because they no longer have any reason for existence.

In city after city, Negroes have gradually become more numerous than whites. Families with higher incomes have moved to the suburbs in an attempt to find the life they once knew. As a consequence, Negroes have won political power in many of these cities. But it is a hollow victory to capture an abandoned city.

America is becoming divided. The rich have no interest in the poor, and the poor have no interest in the rich. Instead, each regards the other as fair game, to be used with whatever weapons are at com-

mand. The battle is far from unequal: The poor
have learned to use the ballot box and the dema-
gogue politician to take the wealth of those they
envy, while the rich resort to government controls
and government contracts as a way to insure a profit.

More mindless still is the small cult of youth, and
its rebellion against authority. As a result of exag-
gerated press coverage, youthful revolt is accepted
as natural, and encouraged as desirable. Some of
our schools teach the young to scorn the values of
society, and propose doubt as a preferable alternative. This cult of youth dooms its flower children to
permanent immaturity, protest, and LSD. Its members are thus destroyed as upright citizens.

Was it for this cult that the Founding Fathers
sought to secure the blessings of liberty?

Our Sense of Purpose

Posterity alone is not the problem. Our nation
itself has doubts about its sense of purpose. Since
the stalemate in Korea, our influence in world
affairs has drained away, even though we have
poured increasing amounts of our resources into
international problems. We refrain from pursuing
our legitimate interests abroad, and we apologize
abjectly for our failures at home. Our children are
learning their lessons too well from their prodigal
elders.

These problems were not those to which the
Founding Fathers looked forward when they sought
to secure for us the blessings of liberty.

The Founding Fathers knew too well the pernici-
ous effects of unbridled government and unbridled
citizenry. Their writings are full of speculations

upon the importance of such problems to society. But their belief was that the Federal Government was best concerned only with the political sector—and that sector was but a small part of life. That is why the sweeping purposes expressed in the Preamble are followed by a coldly practical document that carefully fragments political power.

Those who have tried to alter the Constitution by abandoning its essential spirit, those who have insisted on the short-sighted policy of "bringing it up to date"—in short, all those who have tried to bend the document to passing social concerns or to shallow political philosophies—have tasted the fullness of bitter fruit.

All that the Founding Fathers wanted to do was to ordain and establish a CONSTITUTION. Our problems today began with the tampering of that noble work.

Chapter II

THE FOUNTAINHEAD OF CHANGE

What is wrong?

The trouble began with the attack on the Constitution.

The Constitution is basically the framework of order, and the symbol of law. It is an instrument which enables the nation to defend itself against the enemies of order, whether they come from within or from without. It was designed to protect the people and to preserve their liberties from encroachment.

The assault upon the Constitution today is being led by the Supreme Court. In the name of "interpretation," the Court has rearranged the original meaning and intent of the Framers of the Constitution. The direct effect of the Court's actions in criminal procedure has been to enable criminals and subversives more freedom to destroy our civil order. The indirect effect—assisted by those self-righteous individuals who urge "civil disobedience"—has been a mounting disrespect for the majesty of the law and rightful public authority. Other Court decisions have negated authority of the states, restricted public worship and laid the foundation for a welfare state. Crime in the streets, a free rein for communism, riots, agitation, collectivism and the breakdown of

moral codes, are the fruits of the Supreme Court's
assault on the Constitution.

The Constitution has been under attack for many
years. Quite simply, it was long an obstacle to those
who wanted to change the form of government laid
down by our forefathers. Or, more correctly, the
obstacle was the Supreme Court, supposedly the
guardian of the Constitution and our way of life.

It was no wonder, then, that those who wished to
modify the original intent of the Constitution attacked the Supreme Court. Franklin D. Roosevelt's
attempt to pack the Court in 1937 with a super-
cargo of political puppets is the most notorious
example.

The situation today is different. The most devas-
tating and relentless assault on the Constitution is
coming from the Supreme Court itself. Under the
name of humanity, equality, social welfare or various other pretexts, the Court has been amending
the Constitution by its decisions.

The Judicial Revolution

Although the judicial revolution gained momentum over a long period of time, history will cite one
date as the most conspicuous moment when the
Court freed itself of its oath to uphold the Constitution. The date when that blow was struck was
1954; the case was *Brown v. Board of Education,*
which held that enforced racial segregation in the
public schools of a state is a violation of the equal
protection clause of the Fourteenth Amendment.
Both sides would agree that the practical effect of
the decision was to substitute one idea of the best
kind of social organization for another. Revolu-

tionary social change was instituted without reference to the desires of the electorate. What was legal and constitutional one day was "illegal" and "unconstitutional" the next.

Understandably, passions still run high on both sides of the question. At heart, the issue was not a simple legal adjustment, but a deep political question, that has torn this nation repeatedly from the beginning. Those who have sought to promote revolutionary social changes, contrary to the wishes of the people, have always come up against the barrier of the Constitution.

Exactly one century before the *Brown* decision, the Dred Scott case had also come before the Supreme Court. When that decision was handed down three years later (1857), it was clear that the Constitution barred any revolutionary changes imposed by the Federal Government. Moreover, it is no exaggeration to say that the War between the States was brought on because the social revolutionaries refused to stop at the constitutional barrier cited by the Supreme Court.

One other point is highly significant. The Dred Scott decision was, in effect, superseded by the Fourteenth Amendment. Even though the Fourteenth Amendment was legislated and imposed by force of arms, its partisans still felt that an actual Constitutional amendment was needed to preserve the outward appearance of legality.

However, in the *Brown* decision of 1954, the Court discarded the amending process entirely; henceforth, it would be necessary only to "interpret" the words of the Constitution in the light of modern "findings." Proponents claimed the Constitution should be a "living document." The intent of the

Framers of the Constitution and previous judicial decisions could be ignored. The Constitution would have whatever meaning could be derived from the words—as long as the meaning fit the political philosophy of five Supreme Court Justices.

In 1967, the judicial revolution came full circle with the appointment of Thurgood Marshall as Supreme Court Justice. Marshall was well-known as the chief advocate in the *Brown* case; but he was also well-known as a leading advocate of the theory of the "living document." Given the philosophical composition of the Court in 1954, it is difficult to imagine any other outcome for the *Brown* case, whether Marshall had played a part in it or not. Nevertheless, Marshall was the symbol of the judicial revolution, and his appointment was clearly symbolic of the Court's usurped role. In that new role, the Court becomes an advocate, instead of a judge.

Judge Marshall summed up this role, frankly, when his nomination came before the Senate Judiciary Committee. He said: "You can't expect the Court to apply the Constitution to facts in 1967 that weren't in existence when the Constitution was drafted."

A greater modification of the role of justice could not be imagined. The function of a court is precisely to apply unchanging law to a set of facts which were not in existence when the law was framed. Laws by their nature lay down general principles simply because legislators are aware that they cannot foresee particulars that have not yet taken place.

If the Constitution is truly a "living document," then there would seem to be little reason to breathe new life into it with every generation. For those who make such a claim, the Constitution lives only in their imaginations.

Here is a partial record of the mortal blows which the Supreme Court has been dealing the Constitution since the *Brown* decision:

CRIMINAL PROCEDURE

Mallory v. U.S., 1957. Even though the defendant voluntarily confessed to rape, the Court freed him because he was not taken to a magistrate for arraignment soon enough. The Court held that in federal criminal prosecutions, officers must not try to get a voluntary confession from a suspect until he has been formally charged, told of his rights to counsel, his right to silence and that what he says will be used against him. This decision practically eliminates getting voluntary confessions in federal prosecutions.

Escobedo v. Illinois, 1964. The defendant was convicted of murder on the basis of a voluntary confession. Because the defendant was not allowed to have his lawyer present during police questioning, the confession, even though voluntary, was held inadmissable in court. On this decision the Court split five to four. Justice White, in a dissenting opinion, sums up the damaging effect of the *Escobedo* verdict: "The decision is thus another major step in the direction of the goal which the Court seemingly has in mind—to bar from evidence all admissions obtained from an individual suspected of crime, whether voluntarily made or not . . . [law enforcement] will be crippled and its task made a great deal more difficult, all in my opinion, for un-

sound, unstated reasons, which can find no home
in any of the provisions of the Constitution."

Miranda v. *Arizona,* 1966. In another split decision, the Court considered four criminal cases on
appeal. In one, Miranda, 23 years old, confessed
to the kidnaping and rape of an 18-year-old girl
near Phoenix, Arizona. His voluntary confession,
including a description of the crime, was made to
police during a two-hour interrogation. The Supreme Court overruled his conviction. The Court
extended the *Escobedo* ruling, holding that once a
defendant is in the custody of police, he must be
informed of his right to have his lawyer there, and
if he is indigent, that one will be appointed for him.
Further, that the police must ask no questions of
the defendant if he says he does not want to answer
their questions or that he wants a lawyer present.

Justice White, in a strong dissent, stated: "In
some unknown number of cases the Court's rule
will return a killer, a rapist or other criminal to the
streets and to the environment which produced him,
to repeat his crime whenever it pleases him."

He noted further: "The easier it is to get away
with rape and murder, the less the deterrent effect
on those who are inclined to attempt it."

Berger v. *New York,* 1967. The defendant was
convicted of conspiracy to bribe the chairman of the
New York State Liquor Authority, based upon evidence obtained by electronic eavesdropping. Justice
Black, certainly no conservative, stated in his dissenting opinion: "It is stipulated that without this
evidence a conviction could not have been obtained,
and it seems apparent that use of that evidence
showed the petitioner to be a briber beyond all
reasonable doubt."

Yet the Court reversed the conviction on the grounds that this constituted unreasonable search and seizure.

CIVIL RIGHTS

Heart of Atlanta Motel v. *U.S.*, 1964. Reversing a precedent of 81 years standing, the Court held that Congress had the power to regulate private business practices with the Civil Rights Act of 1964. Previous decisions had held that this Act's "Commerce Clause" did not grant such extensive powers to Congress.

Reitman v. *Mulkey*, 1967. California voters overwhelmingly approved an amendment to that state's constitution which would have prohibited their legislature from passing a so-called "open housing" statute. The Supreme Court declared the amendment void.

PRAYER AND THE BIBLE

Engel v. *Vitale*, 1962. In New York State school children recited the following prayer each morning: "Almighty God, we acknowledge our dependence upon Thee, and we beg Thy blessings upon us, our parents, our teachers and our Country."

Any child was free to remain silent or to be excused.

The Supreme Court held this was unconstitutional under the First Amendment's prohibition against laws "respecting an establishing of religion or prohibiting the free exercise thereof. . . ."

Abington School District v. *Schempp*, 1963. The Court extended the prayer ban to include all Bible reading or prayers that constitute a religious exercise, even though participation is voluntary.

COMMUNISM AND SUBVERSION

Pennsylvania v. *Nelson,* 1956. The Smith Act, designed to protect this nation from Communist subversion, is codified under Title 18, U.S. Code, which contains the following clause: "Nothing in this title shall be held to take away or impair the jurisdiction of the courts of the several States under the laws thereof."

Nevertheless, the Court held in effect, that antisedition laws in forty-two states were invalid because Congress, by enacting a statute on this subject, had preempted the field.

Kent v. *Dulles,* 1958. The Court, in another five to four decision, held the Secretary of State does not have the authority to deny a passport to a Communist.

Albertson v. *Subversive Activity Control Board,* 1965. The Court held that since registration as a Communist might be used as an investigatory lead, the Fifth Amendment prevents the government from requiring registration of Communists. Having previously declared State anti-sedition laws invalid, the Court then made this important provision of the federal anti-subversive act ineffective.

U.S. v. *Robel,* 1967. The Court held that the right of association voided the federal law designed to prevent Communists from working in defense plants. The Court, which was divided again, refused to view membership in the Communist Party in any different light from other political activities.

Whitehill v. *Elkins,* 1967. A Maryland law required a teacher to take an oath that he was "not engaged in one way or another in the attempt to overthrow the government of the United States, or the State of Maryland, or any political subdivision of either of them, by force or violence." Further provisions used the terms "destroy or alter" and "by revolution, force or violence." The Court said that a person who believed in altering the government by revolution could believe in peaceful revolution, so the oath was invalid.

STATES' RIGHTS

Baker v. *Carr,* 1962. The Supreme Court had traditionally refused to get into apportionment of state legislatures, considering it a political matter. This case held that the Court had jurisdiction in this field.

Reynolds v. *Sims,* 1964. On the principle of one-man-one-vote, the Court held that both houses of state legislatures must be based on population (in spite of the fact that Congress itself served as the guide for the system long used in most states).

Harper v. *Virginia Board of Elections,* 1966. The Court, in a six to three decision, held that states could not require payment of a poll tax as a prerequisite to voting. Justice Black, in his dissent, stated: "It seems to me that this is an attack not only on the great value of our Constitution itself, but also on the concept of a written constitution which is to survive through the years as originally written unless changed through the amendment process which the framers wisely provided."

Impact and Reaction

Public reaction to these decisions has not been directed so much to the outcome of the particular cases as to the precedents they have set, and the sweeping effects upon current law. The Court was not ruling upon ambiguous points in the law or the Constitution; the Court was making up whole new interpretations of the Constitution which had never before existed. Many of these decisions have been manifestly contrary to the intent of the Framers, both of the Constitution and its amendments; others are reversals of decisions already handed down.

As early as 1958, this new direction of the Court was so apparent that the chief justices of thirty-six of the State Supreme Courts, in an official report, chastised the U.S. Supreme Court for abusing the power given to it by the Constitution.

The duty of an appellate judge is, of course, somewhat different from that of a trial judge. An appellate court—and the Supreme Court is the highest of appellate courts—is designed to correct errors of law, or errors in the application of the law to the particular set of facts established on trial. Appellate courts are not fact-finding bodies, at least not so far as the facts of the particular question before it are concerned. The only extent to which they are obligated to find facts is in determining the intent of Congress in passing a particular law, or enacting a particular constitutional provision.

The weight or preponderance of historical evidence is decisive, and should be controlling in interpreting and applying constitutional concepts to modern-day facts. An appellate judge is not at liberty to tamper with the facts surrounding the approval of a law or constitutional provision, any more than he is at liberty to tamper with the facts established at the trial court level. The notion that a written body of laws undergoes a metamorphosis with time is a notion which leads to the destruction of the basic principle of our government: Ours is a government by law, rather than by man.

As decision after decision has hacked away at this basic principle, responsible criticism has continued to come from all parts of the country. Consider, for example, just four newspaper editorials from major cities:

New York Daily News, September 28, 1966: In "Thank the Supreme Court," the editor tells how a self-confessed child-killer went scot-free, because the District Attorney's only evidence was an inadmissible confession. The woman said, "Thank you, judge." "Thank the United States Supreme Court," retorted State Supreme Court Justice Michael Kern. "You killed the child. You ought to go to jail."

The Detroit News, November 15, 1967: An editorial, "Get Tough or Get Out," quotes Wayne County Circuit Judge E. S. Piggins as saying that the courts "must not lose sight of the fact that society and the complainant have as many rights as the accused." He added, "As a judge, I would be the first to safeguard the rights of the accused, but what about the rights of the citizen who lies in the street with a knife in his back, a bullet in his chest, or a gash in his head?

"Who cries out for him? Society also has Constitutional rights which in recent years seem to have been overlooked or disregarded in favor of the individual lawbreaker."

The State, Columbia, S.C., August 3, 1967: Aptly called, "Judicial Silliness," this editorial noted that the U. S. Court of Appeals in Chicago had ruled that the following "prayer" could not be recited by the kindergarten class at Elkwood Elementary school in DeKalb, Illinois:

> Thank you for the flowers so sweet,
> Thank you for the food we eat,
> Thank you for the birds that sing,
> Thank you for everything.

The reason? The court felt that a Deity was implied in the verse, although the words did not say so.

The Sunday Star, Washington, D.C., March 12, 1967: An editorial entitled, "The Problem—Unequal Justice Under Law," accused the Supreme Court of "Dispensing a brand of justice that is deplorably unequal." It added, "Some people think it is almost subversive to criticize the Supreme Court, and that any criticism must spring from ignorance or malice. Let them read the dissenting opinions of Justices Harlan, Clark, Stewart and White. No more severe condemnations of the majority rulings can be found than those which appear in these dissents. And if the five members in the majority will not heed even these protests of their own brethren, they will have no one but themselves to blame as the Supreme Court and, still worse, the law itself, falls into disrepute."

Why such indignation?

Because proven criminals are freed.

Because subversives are given unlimited access to our society.

Because our children are being deprived of the moral foundation they need to become good citizens.

Because the very foundations of law have been eroded.

No nation can long survive if such conditions are not checked. The Supreme Court is denying this nation the right to survive. It is denying our nation the right to fight effectively against those who would destroy freedom, either for their own selfish interests, or because they hate this country and what it stands for. In establishing the subtle balance between individual freedom and freedom for society as a whole, the Supreme Court has said that society —as organized under the United States Government—cannot win. In the battle for freedom as against license, the Supreme Court has dictated a no-win policy.

The Supreme Court has changed law from something absolute to something relative. It has made law whimsical. It has denied the very essence of law. The chief fountain of lawlessness in this country today is the decisions of the United States Supreme Court.

A criminal is one who sets his own interests above the laws of the nation, without regard to the result; a subversive is one who consciously seeks to tear the very fabric of the nation, whether he acts as part of an alien conspiracy or not. The Supreme Court decisions with regard to crime and subversion must be examined more carefully. Let us first consider crime.

Crime and Disobedience

Some men are under the mistaken assumption that our local policemen keep order. Policemen cannot keep order; every citizen must keep order. The policeman can only deal with the rare exception, the criminal.

The very basis of civilization is voluntary assent to the laws. Every man must freely accept the constraints of law without coercion. To the extent that coercion is exercised or threatened, freedom dies.

Some people think that criminals are only those who break the law for selfish purposes, thereby attacking someone else's rights. Those who think so are mistaken. Criminals are men who break the laws for any reason whatsoever, even if they are protesting what they conceive to be injustice.

Former Supreme Court Justice Charles E. Whittaker said that while some protests are called civil disobedience, they, in reality, are criminal violations.

The American system of government has provided a more flexible system of coping with social change within the framework of the law than any other government on earth. Those who advocate actions outside the law—even for an alleged humanitarian purpose—are attacking the very mechanism that makes the peaceful alleviation of injustices possible.

"Civil disobedience" is an attack on freedom. It encourages citizens to take the law into their own hands. Even when a "civil disobedience" program is aimed at one particular practice, its psychological carryover is distributed throughout the entire system of law. Every law, at some point, is going to contradict the desires of some citizen. If each citizen becomes his own judge, then impartial justice will disappear.

But crime, too, is an attack on freedom. Crime diminishes the freedom of the law-abiding citizen to walk on the streets and to be safe in his home. Crime necessarily calls forth intensified police action by the state. As long as a district has a high crime rate, residents, both innocent and guilty alike, must expect a restriction of their freedoms. Police themselves must respect the letter of the law; but with increased police activity, it is inevitable that more mistakes will occur.

The answer to crime is not simply more police. When whole cities become crime-infested, there can never be enough police. The only answer is more citizen cooperation with police, more support of the local policeman, with greater recognition of the dangerous and courageous job he fills. Above all, there must be less encouragement of "civil disobedience" by the supposed moral teachers of society.

Most often, the call to "civil disobedience" is pressed upon those who suffer severely from the depravations of criminals. It is sad that those who are the victims of criminals are also the victims of false prophets who come to destroy the law.

The entire revolution in criminal law reflects a growing philosophical viewpoint which is based upon the welfare of the person charged with crime, to an almost complete exclusion of a consideration of the welfare of society.

Essentially, this philosophy is based on the idea that society, rather than the individual, bears the responsibility for anti-social or criminal behavior.

The cause of crime is attributed to environment and criminal attitudes attributed to poverty and illiteracy.

This strange idea—that a man is shaped by his physical environment—is incompatible with the idea of freedom. There is no point in having a free government if a person does not believe that man can make free choices. Those who think that poverty creates crime should check the rocketing crime rate in the affluent suburbs, which rose 73.8 percent from 1962 to 1967. Or they should consider the difference in the crime rate between the depths of the depression in 1933 and our present boom of prosperity.

It is not the physical environment that shapes a man, but his moral environment. That is why parents are so concerned about moral education in the schools. Even though the state insists that each child get a proper education, the parent still retains the responsibility to see that the education his child gets is conducted according to the moral principles of the family.

Parents are rightly concerned about who their children's playmates and schoolmates are. They ought to have a right to insist that their children are educated in the traditions and values of their own culture. Above all, they have a right to see that their children are not indoctrinated in a secular, Godless point of view which contradicts the values they are taught at home.

Whenever an adult adopts anti-social attitudes, whether passive or active, he alone must bear the guilt. The end purpose of moral training should be to make the future citizen understand his responsibility. One of the most frustrating results of the trend of recent Supreme Court decisions has been the unequal division of justice between society and the criminal. In effect, these decisions have trampled and degraded the valid and just rights of society, while magnifying and exalting the fictitious and alleged rights of the criminal.

Moreover, these decisions have produced much disarray and confusion in law enforcement and criminal justice procedures, overruling long-established judicial precedents and shackling law enforcement officials. By invoking technicalities and exaggerating civil liberties, the court has permitted many self-confessed and confirmed criminals to be released to prey again upon society.

Consequently, criminals are increasingly defying the law successfully, and public confidence in the ability of our courts to administer justice is being undermined. Even the effectiveness of day-to-day police work has been undermined. In Washington, D.C., for example, police are only able to catch one-quarter of the perpetrators of crimes; a decade ago, the score was one-half.

Studies show that, in civilized countries, at least one person out of twenty will engage in criminal activity. In the United States, the actual crime rate is much higher, rising eight times faster than the population growth during the period 1962-1967. The cause of this discrepancy is the number of repeaters—the same individuals commit crimes over and over again.

This is where the leniency of the courts is shockingly apparent. Only about 1 lawbreaker in 8 is tried and convicted. Of all persons arrested in 1966, seventy-six percent were repeat offenders. The lower courts themselves are to blame for much of this situation, but many good judges are hamstrung by the Supreme Court rulings, chiefly in the famous cases of Mallory, Escobedo, Miranda—names that will live in infamy. Supreme Court decisions not only freed these criminals, but opened the gates to freedom for countless thousands of other vicious men.

Andrew Roosevelt Mallory was freed by the Supreme Court in 1957 because his confession to a rape charge was obtained during "unnecessary delay" in taking him before a magistrate. Three years later he was arrested on a rape-burglary charge. He was later convicted on charges of burglary with intent to commit a felony, assault and battery, and aggravated assault and battery. He was sentenced to 11 to 23 years in prison.

Daniel Escobedo was set free in 1964 by the Supreme Court because he had not been warned of his right against self-incrimination or allowed to consult an attorney before confessing to a murder charge. He has since been arrested several times, most recently on a narcotics charge that brought him a 22-year sentence.

Ernesto Miranda was released by the Supreme Court in 1966 following his conviction on a rape charge because he had not been effectively warned of his right against self-incrimination. He has since been reconvicted on the same charge and sentenced to prison.

What are the fruits of these landmark decisions of the Supreme Court? There are many instances where convictions of hardened criminals have been reversed as a result of these rulings.

In 1965, the manslaughter conviction of Tom E. Alston, Jr., was reversed by the United States Court of Appeals in the District of Columbia, based on the

Mallory rule. He was arrested at 5 a.m., brought to police headquarters at 5:30 a.m. and questioned for five minutes. He denied knowledge of the crime. He then was allowed to speak briefly with his wife and thereafter confessed to the crime. His confession was ruled inadmissible because he was not taken before a committing magistrate "as quickly as possible."

James W. Killough, another Washington man, was convicted in connection with the killing of his wife in 1960. Three times he confessed to the crime, once prior to arraignment, once to a police officer who visited him in jail after the arraignment, and once during a jail classification interview. The first confession clearly was barred by the Mallory rule, and the Court of Appeals ruled out the second as a "fruit" of the first. The third confession also was ruled inadmissible by the Court of Appeals on the ground of implied pledge of confidentiality.

Such decisions cannot be called justice. They are licenses to criminals to continue to thumb their noses at society. They are destroying the basic concept of right and wrong.

Communism

Just as the Supreme Court has struck down the right of this nation to defend itself against criminals, so too it has progressively denied us the ability to defend ourselves against international communism. The right to self-defense inheres in the idea of national sovereignty. It was laid down in the Preamble as one of the purposes of the Constitution. There can be no individual rights or freedoms without national security.

Yet the record of the Supreme Court has been astonishing. From 1919 through 1942, a period of twenty-four years. the Supreme Court accepted jurisdiction in only eleven cases involving communists and their subversive activities. Of these eleven cases, seven were decided against the communist appellants and in favor of the government. In four, the plea of the communist appellant was sustained.

Now the fact that the Supreme Court sustains a communist appellant does not necessarily mean that the Court sympathizes with communist ideology. Any rigorous judge, imbued with a stern understanding and strict interpretation of law, will upon occasion be compelled to pass judgments that are personally repugnant and contrary to his view of what is best for society. However, the Supreme Court is the highest appellate court in the land. In upholding a communist plea, the Court must find the U.S. District Court wrong, the U.S. Department of Justice wrong, the FBI wrong, and the U.S. Congress and its committees wrong.

Since the famous Schneiderman case in 1943, a staggering 147 communist cases have been accepted by the Supreme Court, up to and including *McBride* v. *Smith* (1967). Of these, the Court decided a grand total of 93 *in favor* of the communist plea, and 54 against.

A strict judge, as indicated earlier, sometimes is forced by respect for the law to make decisions which are personally repugnant to him. But precisely those judges who are best known for their cavalier treatment of law, and their elastic concepts of the Constitution, seem to be most anxious to be tolerant of the communists in our midst. The extraordinary number of cases which the Court has accepted in this field, and the monotonous regularity with which anti-subversive laws have been struck down, frequently on the basis of technicalities not germane to the substantive matter of the case, reveal their thinking.

The cumulative effect of these decisions shows that the Court makes no distinction between freedom of expression at home and internal subversive attacks directed by an external enemy. Exhaustive Congressional investigations have found repeatedly that the Communist Party is not an authentic political party. The Internal Security Act of 1950 notes the following legislative findings:

> There exists a world Communist movement which, in its origins, its development, and its present practice, is a world-wide revolutionary movement whose purpose it is, by treachery, deceit, infiltration into other groups (governmental and otherwise), espionage, sabotage, terrorism, and any other means deemed necessary, to establish a Communist totalitarian dictatorship in the countries throughout the world through the medium of a worldwide Communist organization (Sect. 781(1)).

In 1954, Congress passed the Communist Control Act, finding as follows:

> The Congress finds and declares that the Communist Party of the United States, although purportedly a political party, is in fact an instrumentality of a conspiracy to overthrow the Government of the United States. It constitutes an authoritarian dictatorship within a

republic, demanding for itself the rights and privileges accorded to political parties, but denying to all others the liberties guaranteed by the Constitution. . . . The Communist Party is relatively small numerically, and gives scant indication of capacity ever to attain its ends by lawful political means. The peril inherent in its operation arises not from its numbers, but from its failure to acknowledge any limitation as to the nature of its activities, and its dedication to the proposition that the present constitutional Government of the United States ultimately must be brought to ruin by any available means, including resort to force or violence. Holding that doctrine, its role as the agency of a hostile foreign power renders its existence a clear, present and continuing danger to the security of the United States. It is the means whereby individuals are seduced into the service of the world Communist movement, trained to do its bidding, and directed and controlled in the conspiratorial performance of their revolutionary services. Therefore, the Communist Party should be outlawed.

Changes in the world situation since 1954 do not appear to invalidate these findings of law. Whatever the nature of the disputes within the communist bloc, no one has ever suggested that the Communist Party of the United States of America (CPUSA) is anything but a slave of the Moscow line. Indeed, the case is quite the opposite. Both the Executive and Congressional branches of our government have continued to warn of the subversive nature of the CPUSA. The clear warnings of J. Edgar Hoover have not diminished. As recently as February 9, 1967, the Senate Internal Security Subcommittee issued a study whose very title tells the story: "CPUSA—Soviet Pawn."

Only the Judicial branch—that is, the U. S. Supreme Court—has consistently ignored the true nature of communist subversion. The Court appears to draw no distinction between the Communist Party, which serves as a front for the broad network of political operations conducted by the communist apparatus, and political parties which operate within the Constitutional framework. The Court apparently sees no difference between conscientious dissent and a well-financed international conspiracy whose avowed intention is to destroy us from within.

Only the most naïve believe that all communists are open and acknowledged members of the Communist Party, USA. In many respects, the open members are the least effective and least important participants in the conspiracy. The true test of membership is whether a person accepts discipline from the Soviet apparatus; many such persons are forbidden to take part in visible Party affairs. In addition there are those who are too erratic or self-centered to accept discipline from anyone, but who are willing to cooperate consciously with our nation's enemies.

Therefore, laws which seek to control acknowledged members of the Communist Party are dealing only with the most obvious and most easily defined part of the problem. Such laws constitute the bare minimum that a nation can do for survival. It cannot be said that such laws go "too far." They barely touch the surface. In this light, the action of the Court in striking down a requirement that the self-admitted and notorious head of the Communist Party, USA register as a foreign agent, takes on a more menacing aspect.

Moreover, such decisions have made the work of the communists within the civil rights movement much easier.

From the very beginning, the communists have sought a dominant role within the revolutionary movement in the United States. They made common cause with radical socialists and others seeking to change the fabric of society and the restraints of Constitutional government.

Chapter III

BIG GOVERNMENT, BIG DEBT, BIG POWER

During the past twenty years, Americans have enjoyed a steady growth in national income and gross national product. Population has expanded and shifted, creating new social and domestic issues. Through it all the United States has shouldered the burdens of world leadership. All levels of the government—particularly the Federal Government—have been faced with an increasing number of difficult problems.

Under these circumstances, few would argue that the Federal Government must be modern and alert to change. Many Americans, however, do object to the size of the central government, the course it has been taking, what it has done, and what it has failed to do.

Big Government

The size of our present government endangers individual freedom. It has extended the scope of its functions deeply into affairs that once were considered the exclusive sphere of the individual. History shows that there is no limit to the public acceptance of free services paid for by the public treasury—central control notwithstanding. That is one of the dangers of democracy. The more the citizen in a democratic society accepts government subsidies and handouts, the fewer rights he retains for personal choice. When the people learn that they can vote themselves a share of the public treasury, they frequently elect the candidates promising the most benefits as their due, and regularly return the benevolent government officials back to power. The end result is greater centralization of power, leading eventually either to dictatorship or welfare statism.

More and more people are feeling the muscle of federal control exerted by every federal dollar. For example, when the Federal Aid Highway Act was passed in 1956, the provisions for beautifying the highways and controlling billboards were left to the states. Yet in the 1966 amendment, which was sponsored by the Administration, a higher federal share of the construction cost of the highways was provided to a state that agreed to control outdoor advertising on land along interstate highways. Another example can be found in the federal requirement for local schools and hospitals to integrate their facilities or lose their federal aid dollars—even though no racial discrimination might exist.

Some recipients of federal dollars were even cajoled and coerced into supporting an incumbent president in past presidential elections. The federal dollar is being used today as never before to perpetrate the will of Washington bureaucrats—unfortunately, the federal dollar touches every facet of life in America.

Never has there been a nobler experiment in individual freedom than the democratic form of government in the United States. For this we can thank our Founding Fathers, the Constitution they created, and the measures they provided for its preservation. The sagacity of these men has not diminished with time. They worked from a sense of history; they knew the pitfalls of self government and how difficult it would be for the self-governed to "secure the blessings of liberty."

Ben Franklin warned, "They that can give up essential liberty to obtain a little temporary safety deserve neither liberty nor safety."

The Federal Octopus

In the span of one generation we have seen a fantastic growth of the Federal Government and the creation of a giant bureaucracy of "planners" who want to run our lives. The sheer size of government is frightening enough, but the growing involvement of bureaucracy with the economy and society of America is more ominous.

The federal octopus is growing faster than the country. In 1967 there were 2.9 million employees on the federal payroll, up ten percent over the previous year. State and local governments have grown along with the central government—they had to, otherwise they would have been overwhelmed by "do-gooders" from Washington.

By 1967, there were so many government employees that one out of every six workers in the country was working at some level of government. This is twice the ratio of fifteen years ago. Employment by the Federal Government was so high that in thirty of the fifty states, federal workers outnumbered state government workers.

In this rush to create new federal agencies, Washington planners were a little mixed up. The bureaucrats in the old offices found ways to preserve their own empires and remained a part of the federal snowball. As a result, state and local employees are hard put to find the right Washington office with which to do business. For example:

— In the war on poverty, 16 separate departments administer more than 260 programs.

— Over 30 federal programs are concerned with teacher training.

— Five federal agencies are involved in community planning.

— More than 40 different federal programs provide aid for urban development.

On a fiscal year basis, during the twenty-year period from 1947-1967 the population of the United States expanded from 144 million to 200 million. The gross national product (GNP)—that is, the total market value of goods and services produced by the nation—rose from $234 billion to $712 billion. Any comparisons of federal spending are misleading unless they take the population growth and increased GNP into account. The fairest way to compare 1947 to 1967 is to look at things on a per capita basis—how much the government has cost each individual in the country.

Here are some comparisons during the twenty year period:

Federal spending rose from $249 per person to $813 per person.

The cost of government for each citizen rose from $270 to $782. This was an increase of 190 percent.

The annual rate of Federal spending quadrupled—from $36 billion in 1947 to $161 billion in 1967.

On the basis of percent of the Gross National Product, federal spending increased from fifteen percent to twenty-one percent.

The national debt increased by $69 billion.

Taxes and government receipts at the state, local and national levels now account for thirty-five percent of the national income. A recent study of the effect of this showed that about $1 out of every $5 spent for goods and services was spent by the government. About $1 out of every $4.50 of personal income in the United States comes from direct government payments.

Most of this government spending is by the Federal Government. It now supplies state and local governments with thirteen percent of their revenues in the form of federal aid programs. In 1966, these federal aid programs totaled $12.8 billion (not including social security payments). This was up two hundred and sixteen percent over the $4 billion paid in 1957, and it was an increase of eighteen percent over payments in 1965.

There has been a great increase in legislative activity in the Congress. A joint congressional committee study in 1967 showed that in 1966, a total of 18,522 bills were introduced in the House of Representatives and 3,931 in the Senate. Collectively, members of recent Congresses have had to schedule as many as 110,000 appointments for committee meetings in both Houses. Members of the Senate alone had 33,500 committee meetings to fit into their appointment schedules. A typical Senator had 400 to 500 committee meetings to attend. One busy Senator had 737 meetings scheduled, which is the equivalent of a committee meeting of some kind every day, including Saturdays, Sundays and holidays, for a period of two years.

This rise in legislative business has been paralleled by a striking increase in assistance given to constituents. Most of these requests come from people who just cannot figure out how to deal with the great bureaucracy of Washington and all of its red tape. It is no secret that the size and complexity of government has become so great in the past twenty years that Congressional offices are the only authorities close enough to the people to intercede on their behalf.

The Federal Government owns one-third of all land in the United States. Some land ownership at all levels of government is necessary and desirable for government operations and public safety. But one-third of the country is far too much. Government-owned land is tax exempt. Removal of land from the tax rolls of local government takes away a source of local income, and makes the community dependent on other and higher levels of government for operating revenues.

Big Debt

The bigness of government is not confined to the number of employees or the extent of its agencies, buildings or the amount of its land. Of equal, if not more importance, is the cost of running this great establishment, and the fact that each day we go deeper into debt in the process.

The national debt was $352 billion as of March 1, 1968. The interest on this huge sum runs about $40 million a day; if we started to pay off the debt at the rate of $1,000 a minute it would take almost 700 years. Yet almost each year Congress raises the debt ceiling and blithely undertakes some new program upon which to spend even more money. This kind of fiscal irresponsibility creates a credibility gap that makes it difficult to believe that the government is serious about cutting spending.

Another kind of irresponsibility is evident in the trade gap.

In 1966, the United States balance-of-trade took a startling change: For the first time in recent history, our trade went into the red. The United States began importing more goods than it exports.

Unfortunately, the sobering news of our trade deficit had been withheld from the business community and the people at large. The U.S. Department of Commerce was publishing misleading trade statistics, thus covering up an alarming development.

The credibility gap in trade statistics has only recently come to light. The Commerce Department's statistics show that in 1966 United States exports amounted to $29.42 billion, while imports were $25.65 billion. Those figures suggest that the United States had a trade *surplus* of $3.77 billion.

In actual fact, however, the Commerce Department deliberately includes exports authorized un-

der governmentally subsidized programs, such as
Public Law 480 for shipments of food. Payments
for such shipments are nominal, and cannot be con-
verted into dollars. In fact, payments consist of
credits of the purchasing country and can be used
only in that country. No reputable business accounting method would include free samples in reports
of yearly sales. Yet the Commerce Department in-
flates the statistics of hard commercial sales with
giveaways. A realistic accounting reduces the actual
total of exports by ten percent.

On the other side of the balance, the Commerce
Department undervalues imports. It consistently
reports import values on the basis of free-on-board
(f.o.b.)—that is, the cost of the goods when put
on shipboard at a foreign port. The reports of
nearly every other country in the world realistically
include the insurance and freight charges that must
be paid when the ship reaches the domestic port. In
the United States, these additional charges must be
paid in dollars that leave the country. When imports
are figured on a true cost-insurance-freight basis
(c.i.f.) the costs go at least ten percent higher.

When these two adjustments are taken together,
they constitute an error of twenty percent. Instead
of the favorable trade balance of $3.77 billion re-
ported by the Commerce Department, the 1966
trade *deficit* was $1.8 billion. The Commerce De-
partment figures conceal not only a bad trade picture, but also help to obscure an important reason
for our unfavorable balance-of-payments, and the
gold drain.

The Gold Alarm

By early 1968, the news was filled with accounts of the serious depletion of our gold reserves. Foreign banking systems can exchange the dollars they hold for gold, but since 1934 our United States citizens have been forbidden to do so. For a long period of time many foreign banks were insistently demanding gold for the dollars they held.

As long as the international monetary system is in good shape, gold is not necessary for world trade, except for the convenience of transfers of international payments. In ordinary times, the nations demanding gold would be putting themselves at a disadvantage. Dollars can be invested, and bring in a return; whereas, gold cannot be invested, and costs money to transfer and store.

Gold speculators found much to encourage them in their deadly game. The United States was plainly headed for trouble, with few of those responsible for our economic health paying attention to our course. The Administration's request to remove the gold cover was a case in point.

Removing the gold cover is only a short-term answer to a pressing problem. By law, the Federal Reserve was required to maintain a twenty-five percent gold reserve. We always had enough gold on hand so that this restriction never came into effect. The margin of free gold available to meet foreign demand, when the gold cover was removed, was only $1.3 billion—but even half of that was expected to be used up by domestic needs and currency expansion.

Those who argued for the removal of the gold cover said that we are on the horns of an uncomfortable dilemma. They said that if we were to suspend gold payments, a worldwide monetary crisis would ensue. On the other hand, the machinery of the Federal Reserve Act provided for continuing payments to meet foreign demands, even below the gold cover minimum, but with an emergency tax upon the Federal Reserve system. The effect of the emergency clause would have been to raise the discount rate for loans, and depress the domestic economy.

Removal of the gold cover, in effect, meant removal of the emergency mechanism. Like a sick patient anesthetized against pain, the nation no longer could be aware of the true state of our economy. Without stringent measures to reverse the outflow of gold, removal of the gold cover is a dangerous action.

In 1965, Congress partially removed the requirement for a gold cover on Federal Reserve deposits, without taking steps to cure the gold demand. Three years and $5 billion in gold later, we were once more faced with the same issue.

Partial removal of the gold cover in 1965 did not encourage foreign nations to stop cashing in their dollars. Instead, the 1965 action was correctly interpreted as a sign of weakness, and some nations, particularly France, moved in for the kill. The repetition of the same policy in 1968 was interpreted abroad as a sign of fiscal irresponsibility. It served to whet their appetite.

The most important function of the gold cover was to serve as a Congressional statement of policy on the soundness of our fiscal affairs. Its removal further depressed credibility in the Government's will to accept fiscal discipline.

The Hidden Branch of Government

The combination of bureaucratic power grabs has created a hidden "fourth dimension" of government that exerts increasing influence on our private lives. These agencies permit the planners in our country to use their own discretion in deciding who gets public funds and the conditions under which aid will be extended. Control is where the money is. Now this control is with the central government and the bureaucratic planners in Washington.

The situation harkens back to 1776, when one of the grievances of the Declaration of Independence was: "He has erected a multitude of new offices, and sent hither swarms of officers, to harass our people, and eat out their substance."

The twentieth-century composition of "the multitude of new offices" consists of appointed officials and civil service employees—many of whom are loyal, dedicated and sincere, but, who as a group, think they know what is best for the rank and file of the American people. By various means—such as preparation of complicated legislation (which they will implement after enactment), executive order, or the mere establishment of administrative policy—they are able to circumvent the voting public and impose their own ideas and concepts. This group is particularly adept at prescribing sweeping policies, and using the "shotgun" approach to problems, even though it is often far wiser to examine the problem at local levels. Take air pollution, for example.

Air pollution is commonly cited as a problem which demands cooperation at all levels of government. As it is, only the Federal Government has the power to regulate the manufacture of automobiles to reduce air pollution from engine exhaust. But the states and local communities can do a lot to regulate other local producers of polluted air—industrial wastes, public incinerators, even the burning of leaves. In addition, the problem varies greatly from state to state. The residents of smog-bound Los Angeles are much more concerned with air pollution than, for example, residents of North Dakota where the winds change the air every three seconds.

Government by Guideline

There is an alarming trend toward "government by guideline" today. This means that people are ruled more and more in their daily lives by the unilateral decision of some bureaucrat or appointed official, instead of by legislation framed by their elected representatives.

A current ruling of the Federal Trade Commission established a precedent which threatens to give government the power to regulate advertising practices of magazines and newspapers. For years it was an accepted practice in the trade to give volume discounts based upon the amount of advertising space purchased. The Federal Trade Commission declared that this gives unfair advantage to companies who advertise the most. Of course, the FTC has no power to *control* the *volume* of advertising at all. It just assumed the power, and justified the seizure on the strength of its mandate in anti-trust legislation.

In another arena the Federal Communications Commission, which has no specific mandate to control advertising, some time ago renewed the licenses of several Florida broadcasters with the proviso that the stations report the number of advertisements carried. The Commission further required the stations to explain the unusual concentration of commercials. The FCC officials tried to justify their power grab on the basis that they were "doing a public service." Apparently they forgot the public had the option of turning the dial. The realities of free enterprise and the discipline of the marketplace are much better monitors of service than federal bureaucrats.

Nothing daunted, the FCC went even further and established regulation of community TV antenna systems. Congress had refused to give the Federal Communications Commission any such regulatory power, but the FCC issued regulations by edict— and in effect told the community antenna TV industry to take it to court if they didn't like it.

Sometimes projects that are worthy in themselves are established in the same kind of unauthorized power grab. In 1966, President Johnson announced that he had directed the Secretary of Health, Education and Welfare to establish a National Center for the Prevention and Control of Alcoholism. At that time legislation to establish such a center was pending in Congress; yet by executive order, the President established the Center without Congressional oversight or debate.

In the same way, the Public Health Service set up the controversial National Clearinghouse for Smoking and Health, with a $2.5 million budget, simply by administrative order. The National

Clearinghouse, set up outside the authority of the people's representatives in Congress, is a propaganda agency directed against the nation's tobacco industry.

The proponents of big government in Congress pushed through a bill to create a public, governmentally financed, educational television and radio corporation. This corporation was to assist and finance the production of educational and cultural programs to be offered free to educational TV stations around the country. For the first time in our history, the government was to be significantly involved in the preparation of programs for viewing by the public. Theoretically, the bill excludes partisan politics, but there is no safeguard against presentation of philosophical or ideological material. Programs can still be slanted by the bias of the officers appointed to direct the corporation. The Board of Directors, once appointed, will be free agents.

Cost Analysis

Another recent development in the federal hierarchy that promises to bring central planning for society to an absurdity is the introduction of former Defense Secretary McNamara's Planning-Program-Budgeting System throughout the executive departments. This is a supposedly objective system of finding least-cost alternatives for different programs. Pseudoanalysts in this business often get carried away and try to "quantify" (assign mathematical values) to program elements that are not subject to that kind of analysis. For example, in Health, Education and Welfare programs, one of the important criteria to be used in estimating social benefits from control of a specific disease will be the dollar value of a worker's time saved (through its control). This could easily build a bias against investment of tax-payers' funds in the control of diseases that have the highest incidence among low-income workers.

In an explanation of the Planning-Program-Budgeting System (PPBS), the *Wall Street Journal* pointed out, "PPBS budgeting will influence such choices as whether $20 million of Federal money would do most against cancer through research for a cure, training of doctors and other programs to secure early detection, or building of new treatment facilities. . . ."

This sort of analysis will give the red tape architects in Washington a great store of official-sounding nonsense to use in exerting control over state and local programs.

Federal System

During the last two years we have heard a great amount of talk about "creative federalism." This is just another term coined to hide the failure of Great Society planners. The President pushed through so much social legislation, and established so many new agencies and programs in 1966, that all levels of government became bogged down with delay, overlap and red tape. Even his friend and ally from Texas, Governor John Connally, brought these complaints to a Congressional hearing about federal-state relationships:

Long delays.

Overuse of general language. (No one in Washington would say "Yes" or "No.")

Lack of priorities or rank in grant applications.

Requirements for comprehensive planning.

Confusion among the agencies in Washington.

Too many "coordinators."

Generally, the bureaucrat is insensitive to the plight of the public, more concerned about his own rights and privileges, and is prone to favoritism. Some are arrogant and aggressive, and constantly seek to enlarge their empires. Others are meek and withdrawn, and tend to pass the buck and do as little as possible. Both types have been successful in perpetuating themselves in paper work.

Recently a Senate Subcommittee asked expert judgment of one hundred and nine Federal aid administrators on a number of questions designed to show their attitudes, operating techniques and relationship with the public. Most were more concerned with the protection of their programs than they were with the needs of the communities they serviced. The responses showed four general behavior patterns:

Functionalism (the protection of the individual's programs)

Professionalism (The commitment to standards of the specialized group to which the Director belonged)

Standpatism (Resistance to change or new ideas)

Indifference ("The cavalier dismissal of serious questions or topics as being irrelevant or unimportant.")

Not all officials are guilty of bureaucratic practices. But history of other civilizations, as well as our own, inevitably leads to the conclusion that static bureaucracy is one of the characteristics of big government. The more power we give to these administrators of our laws, the more they will want. The longer they are permitted to exercise power (which is possible in many ways) the less freedom there will be for the public at large.

Chapter IV

NATIONAL DEFENSE

In January, 1968, most Americans learned for the first time that the United States Navy had a ship named *Pueblo*. It was the *Pueblo* incident which revealed to the world that the United States would suffer unbelievable insult before using force for retaliation.

On the morning of January 23, tight-lipped Navy officials shamefacedly announced that the USS *Pueblo,* a small intelligence-collecting ship with a crew of eighty-three, had been forcibly seized by North Koreans in international waters of the Sea of Japan. As the announcement was made, the *Pueblo* was tied up to a dock in the North Korean port of Wonsan, and her crew was in captivity.

Across the land there was a stunned first silence, followed by a groundswell of disbelief and anger. The people of the United States and the world waited breathlessly for the awful retribution that the United States would visit upon North Korea for its irresponsible act.

They waited, and waited, and waited.

Hindsight investigation revealed that the *Pueblo* seizure could and should have been avoided. The small ship fairly bristled with new and sophisticated listening equipment. In her crew there were some of the Navy's most highly trained technicians for this specialized work. In short, the *Pueblo* was a valuable prize, capable of performing excellent "ferret" work in intercepting communications. Her loss meant incalculable damage to our intelligence collection forces.

Pueblo was worth the effort necessary to guarantee her security. Emergency plans for air support or surface escort could have been prepared.

But—no escorts were provided and no plans were made for contingencies. Why?

The Johnson-McNamara-Rusk regime had so centralized civilian control in Washington that military units worldwide danced like puppets at the end of a long string from the White House.

By even the most conservative estimates, the Administration had almost three hours in which to save the ship. During this time there were United States aircraft and South Korean aircraft minutes away from Wonsan.

Time delay, slow reaction, and a complicated chain of command took their toll. The news didn't filter through to the President until two and a half hours had elapsed. Authority for the use of force had to come from Washington, but Washington was asleep.

The opportunity to avoid *Pueblo's* capture lost irrevocably, President Johnson now had the choice of moving quickly, positively and forcefully to obtain the immediate release of the ship and crew, or to take the cautious route of diplomatic negotiations. He chose the latter course, and sought a solution in the United Nations.

A hesitant Soviet Union, at first aghast at the effrontery of her militant satellite, soon sensed that once again the United States had failed to meet the challenge. Instead of a military ultimatum and a demand for instant return of the ship and its crew, President Johnson sought "to talk his way out of trouble."

Communist bloc nations, elated with this turn of events, used the incident to great propaganda advantage, deepening the shame and humiliation of the American people.

Amateurs at the Helm

Meanwhile, the United States continued a protracted war in Vietnam where American casualties total about 23,000 dead and 140,000 wounded. Over a half-million men are bogged down in this no-win conflict that has been masterminded by civilians. Our military forces around the world are stretched thin, and our nuclear superiority *vis à vis* the Soviet Union is going down the drain. Many of our allies are having second thoughts about the credibility of the United States as a military partner.

They are not alone. An angered public is fed up with mistakes, excuses and frenzied efforts of those in power to pass the buck and run for cover when setbacks occur.

Therefore, as the curtain lowers on the eight-year Democratic regime of the 1960's, the American people can remember this period of history as one that began with the Bay of Pigs and ended with the *Pueblo*. In between there was little to applaud and much to regret. For example—

The Cuban Crisis. A hollow victory. Castro still controls Cuba and Soviet missiles are still in Cuban underground sites.

The War in Vietnam. This war bogged down, with unnecessary delays and excessive casualties, because of restrictions and tight control of military operations by the White House.

Nuclear Strategic Balance. The most dangerous mistake of all. From a three to one advantage in total megatonnage delivery capability in 1962, the United States slipped to parity with the Soviet Union in 1967. Projections for 1971 show a Soviet superiority of about two to one.

The ABM. This desperately needed system for home defense was delayed for years, while the Soviets installed their own ABM defenses, tested space weapons, and experimented with the orbital bomb.

Military Muzzling. A Senate investigating subcommittee uncovered Defense Department censorship of anti-communist material from statements and public speeches of military officers. The censorship even extended to the material used in troop discussions and seminars.

The TFX. A six-billion-dollar contract for this controversial aircraft (which is unsuitable in a Navy version) was awarded to the high bidder by the Secretary of Defense. He overruled unanimous military judgment as well as cost analysis, in doing so.

Managed News. One of the reasons for the
credibility gap with the Administration. Defense claims the right to lie to the public, military news has been distorted and unnecessarily
withheld; on occasion it was used for political
advantage.

It took a war in Southeast Asia and some spec-
tacular Soviet missile and space achievements to
bring this country to its senses with regard to national defense. The case against Secretary Mc-
Namara was coming to a head when President
Johnson tactfully relieved him. The first sign of
serious military dissent occurred in the August 1967
hearings before the Senate Preparedness Investigating Subcommittee. These were followed by Mc-
Namara's reversal of position on the ABM, and
Congressional hearings on the TFX project. House
committees criticized military procurement, and
called the M-16 rifle situation a "scandal." The
documentation against Defense policies was reaching the explosion point in the fall of 1967.

During the hearings on the conduct of the air
war in Vietnam, military leaders surprisingly were
allowed to express their true opinions to the Senate committee without fear of retaliation. The unanimous disagreement of military commanders with the
conduct of the war brought latent discord between
top military and civilian personnel to the surface.
Soon afterward, Soviet developments with their own
anti-missile defense and the orbital bomb uncovered
the nakedness of United States defenses and revealed
deficiencies in our own strategic arsenal. The conse-
quent alarm and expressions of public dissatisfac-
tion brought about the long-needed change in civilian

leadership at the Pentagon—hopefully in time to repair the damage.

The seven-year tenure of Secretary McNamara was marked by the arrogant substitution of clever management techniques over military training and experience in military matters. Competent military planning was delayed and thwarted by over-analysis. Military operations were closely controlled by amateurs in Washington. This started during the Cuban crisis and reached its peak in Vietnam where, for a while, the President selected specific targets for tactical bombing. Civilians would prescribe the weapon load for the aircraft, and tell pilots the tactics they were to use in carrying out their missions.

The principle of civilian control of the military, to which all military officers subscribe, does not mean over-control and super-direction of military operations from the seat of the government. This is patently wrong and inherently disastrous. It has led to the use of military power as a means to signal political intentions to the enemy during combat operations. This practice alerts the enemy, causes heavier casualties and hamstrings our operating forces.

Few would argue that it is sound to use the deployment and increased readiness of military power as signs of national intent prior to the commencement of hostilities. It is entirely different, however, to continue that policy after the fighting has begun. Once hostilities start, the military professions should be allowed to conduct their operations with a minimum of long-distance guidance. Given broad objectives and policies from the Commander-in-Chief, military commanders can carry out campaigns with economical use of forces and minimum casualties. But when they are hampered by nit-picking, detailed orders and constraints, when their operations are conducted as much for political effect as for destruction, their campaigns drag out and casualties mount.

Vietnam

The management of the war by amateur civilian "experts" has been botched badly.

The fruits of civilian mismanagement of the war in Vietnam are bitter. In addition to the mounting casualty lists, deep schisms at home, loss of face throughout the world, and derision from some former allies for our plight, we must face the fact that the country has not geared itself to conduct a major war.

The policy of "gradual" escalation that we have so unwisely followed in Vietnam is like a bottomless pit. It is contrary to good military practice, it is costly and it is indecisive. It gives the initiative to the enemy.

The basic mistake of the conduct of the war was the President's refusal to accept the recommendations of the Joint Chiefs of Staff (JCS). These men —the product of years of experience, training and selection—are among the best of the armed forces. The incumbents during the buildup in Vietnam from 1965 to 1967 were: General Earle Wheeler, Chairman; General Harold Johnson, Chief of Staff of the Army; Admiral David McDonald, Chief of Naval Operations; General John McConnell, Chief of Staff of the Air Force; and General Wallace Greene, Commandant of the Marine Corps. The combined military experience of these men totals one hundred and eighty years, fifty of which were in combat. They have spent their lives to learn their military profession, yet, in decision after decision on Vietnam, they were overruled by the Secretary of Defense and the President. For example:

The Joint Chiefs of Staff recommended a rapid buildup in 1965 when the decision was made to send American combat units into Vietnam—400,000 men in the first six months. They were overruled.

The JCS recommended a paralyzing air campaign at the outset to gain momentum and to keep the advantage. They were overruled.

The JCS recommended the call up of the National Guard and reserves in 1965 in order to win quickly in Vietnam and to keep our guard up elsewhere. They were overruled.

Consequently our military strength around the world has suffered, the war has dragged on, casualties have soared, and our men are being killed with weapons supplied by the Soviet Union and Red China.

For three years the JCS and other top military leaders unanimously recommended closing the port of Haiphong, and the other smaller ports of North Vietnam, where eighty-five percent of the modern artillery, tanks, fighter aircraft, radar, missiles, helicopters and ammunition—almost all of the sinews of war—are imported.

The ports are still open.

The forces in Vietnam led by General William Westmoreland have fought a kind of war never seen before in the history of armed conflict. The military commanders have been subject to the directions of amateur strategists—civilians in the higher levels of the Administration with no military experience and little responsibility. This is not the kind of civilian control envisioned by our forefathers. This is out and out meddling, and contrary to the advice of a report of the Senate Armed Services Committee that was issued in 1962 after the Cuban crisis:

> "If war should come, it can be conducted successfully only by military professionals in that art, and if strategy or tactics come under the direction of unskilled amateurs, sacrifice in blood is inevitable and victory is in doubt."

Later another report—this one from the Senate Preparedness Investigating Subcommittee—pointed out, after hearings on the air war in Vietnam, that:

> "Every military witness who testified emphasized that the air war had been waged under severe handicaps which were contrary to military principles. Complex and complicated rules and controls, plus the necessity to obtain approval in Washington for even relatively insignificant actions and tactics, have been the order of the day."

The former Deputy Commander of the 7th Air Force in Vietnam, Major General Gilbert L. Meyers, said in connection with these restraints and ground rules: "We were literally fighting with one hand tied behind our back."

As a result of these hearings the situation has improved, but as late as March, 1968, the following restrictions were in effect:

The United States will not undertake any steps to overthrow the government of North Vietnam.

United States aircraft are not permitted to strike any target within five miles of Hanoi, or three miles of Haiphong, without special permission in each case.

United States aircraft cannot cut rail lines in the vicinity of the Red Chinese border, even though it is North Vietnamese territory and not Chinese.

United States aircraft and ships are forbidden to mine the major North Vietnamese ports, including Haiphong, through which most of the enemy supplies are brought in.

United States ships may not bombard any shore installations that are within a line sixty miles south of Hanoi.

United States aircraft may not strike targets in populated areas.

During the 1968 TET offensive, the North Vietnamese demonstrated by their attacks on South Vietnamese cities, that they have no compunctions about civilian population, nor do they have any arbitrary sanctuaries.

The inefficiency of long-range, civilian control of Vietnam operations was not limited to the air war. The Gulf of Tonkin incident was another example. During the engagement of August 4, 1964, the commanding officer of one of the destroyers was overwhelmed with high priority messages from Washington. Message after message arrived, asking for irrelevant details and demanding an immediate answer. It became so bad the skipper's unit commander on the scene had to come to his rescue. In a most welcome bit of advice he said: "Fight, don't write."

Later, it was said of this engagement: "Never before in military operations have so many directed so few."

It is time to let our military commanders all over the world have the authority to fight (and not write) when the situation calls for it. That policy would have saved the *Pueblo*.

It is quite popular to call those who advocate strong policies, "warmongers." It is not warmongering to insist on the best leadership for the youth of our country who are serving in the armed forces. It is not warmongering to demand tactics that save lives. On the other hand it is a tragic mistake to get our military men involved in untenable situations where they incur high casualties and not give them the leadership and freedom of action to win.

What good does it do to contribute the majority of our national income to the maintenance of forces that we are afraid to use? We are a great, strong nation, whose retaliation to insult and aggression should strike fear into the hearts of any aggressor anywhere in the world. Yet we are like a giant with an Achilles heel. The weakness lies in our leadership, which revels in self-pity and glories in exhibitions of unnecessary restraint.

These are the men who have made the United States appear ridiculous in the eyes of the world, the men who are unwilling to uphold the honor and dignity of our flag, who participate in no-win wars, and who permit the capture of a Navy ship on the high seas without immediate retaliation and forceful recovery.

We hear a lot about credibility today. Many believe that our military strength is not a credible deterrent so long as we are afraid to use it properly. For too many years we have been overly obsessed with fear of world censure and the reactions of other nations to our initiatives. Because of this fear-oriented philosophy, we are bogged down in war that is draining away our life's blood. In other areas our military resources are stretched thin, and because of our growing reputation for being a paper tiger, these forces are exposed unnecessarily to aggression and insult.

The decision the American people should make, and make soon, requires a reappraisal of our use of force. We should think of the example of Israel —not Egypt. If a war is worth waging, it is worth winning. We should decide, as quickly as possible, whether we really plan to win this war in Vietnam— if we do, then we should give our military leaders broad guidance and then let them bring the war to a quick, convincing victory.

If we decide against military victory, there should be no half measures—no more gradual escalation, no more managed news and questionable reports of progress. We have had enough of that. Instead, we ought to adopt the military posture of a declining world power—that is, put our tails between our legs and withdraw from Vietnam.

The Nuclear Balance

The defense of the United States against nuclear attack is predicated on taking those measures that will best assure that no enemy will ever unleash the terror of nuclear weapons over this land. In considering this grave question, we cannot afford to make mistakes or to act on false assumptions. For our own safety, security and peace of mind we have to cover all bets—no matter what the cost. First, we have to recognize that the primary opponent is the Soviet Union, and we cannot assume, for example, that the Soviets think as we do, or that they will not follow a certain course because it is illogical. We must realize that in this conflict of the minds, we are playing for keeps.

In the past few years we have witnessed a parade of actions that has changed our strategic policy from one of winning to one of deterring. The theory is that the Soviet Union is mellowing, and that the Soviet leaders will see the folly of spending large sums of money to increase their nuclear missile capability or to bolster their defenses. The policy of deterrence is supposed to reduce international tension and increase stability.

What is the net result of these theories and policies?

In the span of ten years, from 1961 to 1971, the United States and the U.S.S.R. will have reversed their roles as nuclear powers. From a tremendous superiority in delivery capability of nuclear weapons in 1961, the United States slipped almost to parity with the Soviet Union in 1967, and forecasts show a decided Soviet advantage by 1971.

This is calculated in terms of total megatonnage delivery capability—not the number of launchers in place.

The June 1967 report of the House Armed Services Committee, entitled "The Changing Strategic Military Balance U.S.A. vs. U.S.S.R." shows that the United States will have from 6,000 to 15,000 total megatonnage delivery capability in 1971.

Then, the report states, the Soviets will have from 30,000 to 50,000 megatonnage delivery capability.

TOTAL MEGATONNAGE DELIVERY CAPABILITY

U.S.		U.S.S.R.
25,000–50,000	(1962)	6,000–12,000
8,000–29,000	(1967)	16,000–37,000
6,000–15,000	(1971)	30,000–50,000

After projecting these figures, the report concludes with this conservative statement:

> "The preponderance of evidence points to the conclusion that the Soviet Union is succeeding in its massive drive toward strategic military superiority and that the United States is cooperating in this effort by slowing down its side of the arms race."

The men who made that statement were not amateurs. Included in the subcommittee that prepared the report were some of the most experienced strategic experts of our time: Generals Curtis Le May, Bernard Schriever, Thomas Power, Albert Wedemeyer; Admirals Felix Stump, Robert Dennison and Ben Moreell; Dr. Edward Teller and Professor James Atkinson.

The best way to prevent a nuclear war is to maintain a clear nuclear superiority over all world powers capable of launching a nuclear attack against the United States. For the past two decades we enjoyed a favorable balance of power, but were so well-satisfied with our position that we became great philosophers. First, we restricted ourselves

with the "Second Strike" theory. This was suspected
to be our unofficial policy for years, but it was
Secretary McNamara's testimony during the military posture hearings before the U.S. Senate in 1967
that confirmed this. He left no doubt that the military strategy of the United States is based on deterrence through the assured destruction capabilities
after a Soviet first strike.

This is a serious mistake. Even if we never enter-
tained an intention to conduct a preemptive strike,
we should keep that information to ourselves. It
would be far better in the long run to leave the
enemy in doubt. We should make it clear to all
nuclear powers that there might be levels of provocation which would cause us to launch a strike
against their strategic installations. We could back
up that policy with assurances of our ability to
destroy them in a second strike.

At these same hearings, Air Force Secretary
Harold Brown explained the Defense Department's
new theory of deterrence:

> ". . . We have leveled out our missile forces.
> We announced how big our missile force was
> going to be. Our plans are that five years from
> now we will have just as many missiles as we
> have right now. They [the Soviets] have
> known that. They have known that for a couple
> of years, and they keep on building. Now we
> can afford to let them build for awhile, if they
> feel they want to 'catch up.' But there is evi-
> dence that if we stop, they don't necessarily
> stop. They haven't stopped. I think that in our
> position, we can afford to let this go on for a
> while, without over responding."

This was the reasoning and the theory that lost our nuclear superiority. While we delayed urgent programs recommended by the Joint Chiefs of Staff, we signed the Nuclear Test Ban Treaty in 1963, knowing full well that the Soviets were ahead of us in high yield technology. In upper atmospheric tests in 1961 and 1962 the Soviets conducted missile intercepts with nuclear-tipped weapons and learned a great deal more than we know about the mysterious "X-Ray" effect and electromagnetic effects of nuclear explosions in the atmosphere. They developed prototypes of space weapons and experimented with the orbital bomb. While we delayed the deployment of our anti-missile defenses, they proceeded with theirs.

The ABM

At this time there is some disagreement over the extent and capabilities of the Soviet ABM system, but as the American Security Council report put it, "There is no disagreement over the fact that the Russians have something and the United States has nothing."

The same fallacious reasoning that cost us our nuclear superiority was next applied to the "thin" or "Sentinel" ABM system announced by Secretary McNamara in September 1967.

The Sentinel defense being installed to defend against Chinese ICBM's consists of Spartan and Sprint missile systems, controlled by high resolution radar and computer complexes. Fortunately, the component parts for these systems are in advanced stages of development, and the time interval between the "go ahead" and actual installation is much less than it might have been. For this blessing, we can thank the Congress and the JCS, who for years have been recommending development of the ABM. A brief account of their struggle with Defense follows:

Mid 1950's—Each year Congress provided funds for ABM research and development.

1963—In the first secret session of the Senate since World War II, Senators were briefed on our strategic posture and were warned that the Soviets had a prototype ABM system. The Senate Armed Services Committee added an amendment to the annual procurement bill, authorizing appropriation of $196 million to begin procurement of ABM parts. At the instigation of the Administration, this amendment was struck on a roll call vote (58 to 16).

1966—At the insistence of the Senate Armed Services Committee, Congress approved $167.9 million for ABM procurement. Secretary McNamara had not asked for these funds and did not use them.

Nov. 10, 1966—McNamara announced that the Soviets had begun deployment of an ABM system around Moscow.

January, 1967—President Johnson stated that no deployment of a U.S. ABM system would be made until completion of the arms control negotiations with Russia. Secretary NcNamara's military posture report to the Congress contained a lengthy argument against deployment of a complete, Russian-oriented ABM system. He stated that it would be wasteful and ineffective, and it would disturb the strategic balance. Two days later, General Earle Wheeler, Chairman of the Joint Chiefs of Staff, disagreed with the Secretary of Defense, and recommended "a measure of defense" for the country.

1967—Congress approved the following amounts for the fiscal year 1968 military budget:

ABM Procurement .... $297.6 million
ABM R&D .... 421.3 million
ABM Construction .... 64.0 million

June 17, 1967—Red China detonated its first hydrogen bomb. Public pressure for immediate installation of ABM defense mounted.

September 18, 1967—Secretary McNamara announced the decision to deploy a "thin" ABM defense system (the "Sentinel"), oriented against the Communist Chinese threat that would exist by the mid-1970's. He justified this step on the grounds that the Chinese might "miscalculate," but failed to admit that the most dangerous threat to our security would be a similar miscalculation by the Soviet Union.

The Soviet danger is the major threat, and it must be faced resolutely. The Sentinel system is only the beginning, and but a step in the right direction. It is time to listen to the recommendations of the Joint Chiefs of Staff and the more defense-minded members of Congress. For our future peace and security, our ABM defenses should be expanded.

On October 10, 1967, the Outer Space Treaty was ratified by the United States and the Soviet Union. This treaty was designed to bar the orbiting or stationing of weapons in outer space. Less than a month afterward, Secretary McNamara announced that the Soviets were testing an orbital rocket that could bypass our early warning systems by flying altitudes of about 100 miles and using a "backdoor" approach over the South Pole.

As spokesman for the Johnson Administration, Secretary McNamara claimed that the Soviet orbital bomb was not in violation of the Outer Space Treaty, and called the Soviets' move a mistake. The "mistake," according to the Administration view, lies in the fact that an orbital bomb is less accurate than a long-range intercontinental missile, and takes longer to deliver to a target. Earlier, General Wheeler had told the Senate Foreign Relations Committee that, "Weapons in orbit could become a matter of grave consequence, particularly when used in conjunction with other strategic systems."

By developing the orbital bomb, the Soviets are seeking diversification. The Intercontinental Ballistic Missile (ICBM) may be more efficient, but the orbital bomb provides an alternate to their military strategy. A blast from a high-yield orbital weapon may not be accurate enough to destroy our missile sites, but the unknown effects of radiation might wipe out our missile computer memory systems and delicate electronic command and control equipment.

In this regard, we must remember that the Soviets have the advantage of testing nuclear weapons in the upper atmosphere. What little atmospheric test data that we have indicates that the effects of high-yield weapons are radically different from the effects of low-yield weapons. Bigger explosions produce more than a progressively larger increase in effects; the results are mysteriously different.

Here, again, we have a case where the Soviets have something and we do not. It might have been different. In 1963 Secretary McNamara canceled plans for a number of new weapons, including the U.S. version of the orbital bomb. The present charge that the Soviets made a mistake is simply a cover up for that 1963 decision and the faulty reasoning that if we do not develop new weapons systems, the Soviets will not either.

As a consequence, the United States must now proceed with development of a reliable anti-satellite system for use in conjunction with the ABM. The ABM can intercept warheads after they come within range, but a space defense requires long-range tracking systems to calculate orbits and to pinpoint satellites in outer space.

There is still another requirement that must be met. Both the United States and the Soviets are proceeding rapidly with developments of multiple warheads for a single missile. This capability is called MIRV—short for Multiple Independently-Targeted Reentry Vehicle. One bomb can be divided into several missiles, each profiled for a separate target. The best defense against this threat is a "mid-course intercept" weapon system that will destroy the parent missile soon after it leaves the launching pad and before several warheads separate. Present plans of the Air Force and Navy for this capability should be accelerated. Given this ability, we should be able to cut down the number of missiles reaching the United States in a strategic attack. Then there would be less likelihood that our ABM defense would become saturated and have to defend against more missiles than it can handle.

Military Muzzling

The attempt to downgrade military experience and advice first became obvious in 1961 when the Department of Defense, aided and abetted by the State Department, made a concerted effort to eliminate anticommunist themes and phrases from the statements, speeches and articles of military personnel. This drive applied both to the public statements and to the content of the internal military information programs on the cold war. This came to light when high-ranking, patriotic officers of the Armed Services informed certain Congressmen of the general resentment of the military toward the Defense censorship policy.

In extensive hearings by the Senate Armed Services Preparedness Subcommittee in 1962, the details of this oppressive policy were brought to light. The committee members, who were following the usual objective approach of that high body to determine the facts, were incensed to learn that even the testimony of military witnesses appearing before them was being censored by civilians in the Defense and State Departments.

The State Department policy at that time was to treat the continuing struggle of the Communists against the non-Communist world as a "peaceful" competition between nations. This "soft" policy required the elimination of such words as "battle" or "conflict," in favor of softer terms such as "challenge" or "struggle." In some instances, the State Department would eliminate entire sections from speeches of senior officers merely because State censors held different views. For example:

On March 4, 1960, Admiral Arleigh Burke, then Chief of Naval Operations, proposed to say: "We know and the Communists know that they cannot take Cuba by force of arms, but can they take Cuba by intrigue? Could they take Cuba even more readily if our attention was drawn to the Taiwan Straits or to Berlin or to some place else? These are serious things. They are the things we must think about to evaluate the whole threat in its proper context."

At that time it was the enlightened policy of the State Department to regard Castro as an independent revolutionary. The State Department censor eliminated the above material from Admiral Burke's speech, and penciled across the face of the speech an explanation: "Reference to Cuba of this sort, by senior naval officers directly connected with Guantanamo Base, could damage current arrangements for treating Cubans by State."

Other examples of censorship are shown in the following changes of language by Defense and State censors:

Before Censorship	*After Censorship*
1. "And this balanced force of seapower will be able to meet any situation in the spectrum of the cold, the limited, or the general war requirement."	1. "And this balanced force of seapower will be able to meet any situation in the spectrum of the political or military requirement."
2. "One cannot reflect upon these startling facts without considering their influence in our life-or-death competition with the Communists."	2. "One cannot reflect upon these startling facts without considering their influence in our lives today and in the future."
3. "The X-15 is the Man o' War of the stable of research aircraft to date."	3. This was deleted with the comment: "Let's use another steed—Zev, Gallant Fox, etc., but not this one."
4. "Even though this distinction exists, the present state of affairs is nevertheless an actual war."	4. "Even though this distinction exists, the present state of affairs is nevertheless a challenge and a struggle."
5. "As we engage the Communists, let us be fully aware of the significance of the two which are part and parcel of the vicious world-wide conflict forced upon us."	5. "Let us be fully aware of the significance of the two which are part and parcel of our lives and our future."

In another example of fuzzy thinking the State Department refused to let General Carroll, Director of the Defense Intelligence Agency, refer to the Cuban Government as the "Communist Government of Cuba." In a written justification of this censorship the State Department said, "At the time this speech was made, a policy decision had not been made as to whether Cuba should be treated as a Communist government." But this censorship occurred in August 1961, *four months after the Bay of Pigs invasion!*

The official testimony of the muzzling hearings revealed the United States' foreign policy to be as follows: "The U. S. Foreign policy objective is containment of direct foreign military aggression. It does not seek victory over communism, but only to deter aggression while seeking grounds for accommodation, so that the Communist dominated territories will have the necessary time in which to evolve into nonaggressive, socialist states."

As a result of these comprehensive hearings, the State Department and the Department of Defense adopted a more reasonable and responsible policy of clearance, but the obvious insult to intelligence of the military left resentment that smolders to this day.

Miscellaneous Defense Decisions

An indictment of the present Administration's mismanagement of military affairs includes not only those previously mentioned but many others—most of which can be laid at Secretary McNamara's door. Some of these would include his:

1—Stubborn opposition to the installation of nuclear power plants in new construction surface ships.

2—Cutback of manned strategic bombers.

3—Reduction of the Navy's nuclear attack submarine construction program.

4—Arbitrary base closings.

5—Abortive attempt to merge the Reserve and National Guard.

Many other examples of misjudgment could be brought forward but the Johnson-McNamara team will long be remembered for the most publicized boondoggle of all—the TFX.

Johnson's TFX

The celebrated TFX (now called the F-111A for the Air Force, and the F-111B for the Navy) is something that the Johnson Administration will never live down. At the time of the contract award, it was alleged that political and regional pressures influenced the selection of the higher bid. Because the Air Force version was to be built at Fort Worth, Texas, some of the allegations were specifically pointed at Lyndon B. Johnson, then Vice-President, and former Secretary of the Navy, Fred Korth, a banker from Fort Worth.

The $6.5 billion award for the TFX went to the General Dynamics Corporation instead of the Boeing Company, in spite of the fact that the latter had submitted the lower bid and had been the unanimous choice of the Air Force and Navy officers who evaluated the proposals. The reason given was that General Dynamics Corporation had a better plan to capitalize on "commonality" between the F-111A and the F-111B. In retrospect, this was a fatal decision; in effect, it sacrificed weapon superiority for production management efficiency and potential dollar savings.

The F-111A was intended to operate from well-constructed air strips of suitable length, whereas the F-111B was to be a carrier aircraft, subject to the limitations of aircraft carrier short landings and catapult take-offs. Most of the difficulties encountered with the entire program showed up in the Navy version of the aircraft. Defense Department analysts, who were capable of making certainties on paper out of technological uncertainties, and chose to ignore military officer experience and expertise, soon found that the Navy program was in trouble. Production overruns and time slippage were the inevitable result when prototype F-111B aircraft failed to reach performance specifications.

As one admiral put it, "We have permitted the 'maximum commonality' factor to override even the simple necessity of having to get the aircraft on board a ship." As new "fixes" were ordered on the F-111B, the plane became heavier, slower, and less suitable for carrier use. Moreover, the costs skyrocketed from an estimated $2.9 million per copy in 1962 to $10 million each in 1968.

During Department of Defense Hearings for Fiscal Year 1968, Senate members of the Subcommittee on Appropriations brought to light many performance and design deficiencies of the F-111B. One of the more damaging developments was the loss of the characteristics of a fighter aircraft. The Committee report stated:

Defense Department officials now admit that the plane is not capable of dogfighting with enemy aircraft. Although its original designation of TFX represented the words "tactical fighter, experimental" the TFX is no longer a fighter plane. The Navy calls its version a missile-launching "platform," while the Air Force version is considered to be a "low altitude bomber."

In the July 14 testimony, the Navy further admitted that the F-111B will not replace existing fighter aircraft when it goes into service. The F-111B was intended, in 1962, to supplant the F-4 (Phantom) completely as the Navy's carrier-based fighter. Now additional fighters will have to be procured to serve the roles of attack escort and air superiority fighter for which the F-111B was originally intended.

Following up on this point, the report raised the serious question of whether the F-111B was really needed, because of the limitations uncovered. The report said:

The conclusion that we reach about the repeated statements that this plane is urgently required for fleet use by 1970 or 1971 is that testimony about the cost effectiveness study prepared by the Navy for the F-111B is misleading.

Additionally, since F-4s or some other fighter will now be required in addition to the F-111B because of the lack of dogfighting capability in the F-111B, the total fighter-interceptor deck space used will be greater, not less, than that of the present 26 F-4s on a carrier. Thus the F-111B plus supporting fighters will cost more and use more deck space than the present 26 F-4 fighter complement on a carrier. This fact raises questions as to why the F-111B program is being continued.

During later hearings on the Department of Defense budget for Fiscal Year 1969, top Navy admirals reluctantly admitted that the F-111B had become a single mission aircraft, that weight reductions had caused structural weakness. It was too large, too heavy, and too slow. They were so discouraged with the F-111B program that they proposed to "kill" it immediately and divert some of the funds to the development of a lighter, more suitable substitute that could operate from a carrier.

They had fought a good fight with a losing proposition, and had manfully tried to correct the original TFX error that had been perpetrated on the nation's taxpayers. Now, years later and dollars poorer, the Department of Defense faces the stark reality of having to admit failure and bury the Johnson-McNamara billion-dollar blunder.

The Future

The study of history shows that it is essential for a nation to protect itself from the ambitions of covetous rivals. This is particularly true of a nation like the United States that is happily endowed with a great share of the world's blessings. Moreover, history is filled with examples of dictators whose great ambition was to conquer neighboring nations and to extend their borders. The more notable ones were Alexander the Great, Genghis Khan, Napoleon, and Hitler. Today the great dictator is the Central Committee of the Communist Party in the Kremlin.

To defend against the Soviet threat to our security, we should emphasize the maintenance of strong armed forces and a progressive research program that keeps this nation ahead in the technology of new weapons. This is one of the most important duties of the Congress and the voting public. Our survival depends on it.

The threat to our survival demands a national recognition of the global Communist conspiracy. The failure to recognize the Soviet challenge is to repeat the error of the 1930's when the allies refused to believe Hitler's aims and intentions. The Soviet's aims are clearly visible: Great expenditures on nuclear weapons; tremendous development of her Navy, including a giant submarine program; expansion into the Middle East, the Red Sea and the Mediterranean; overt support of North Vietnam and North Korea in the Pacific; the successful attempt to establish missiles in Cuba; and the constant stream of propaganda emanating from Radio Moscow.

In the face of these realities, we should make up our minds to keep our forces strong, to develop the best weapons systems possible, and to revise our policy for using them. We should lift self-imposed restrictions on deployed military units, decentralize authority to our field commanders in matters below the nuclear threshold, and demand respect for our national honor and flag. The tougher we are, the less likelihood the enemy will challenge us. One thing is certain—the more we pursue fear-oriented policies and appear like a paper tiger, the more we will encourage further aggression and insult.

Chapter V

COMMUNISM THROUGHOUT
THE WORLD

On the morning of January 4, 1968, the Soviet freighter *Pereyaslavl-Zalesskiy* was tied up in the Cua-Cam estuary of the port of Haiphong. The cargo of the freighter was being transferred into a light boat which had pulled up alongside. Suddenly, American planes swarmed in for an attack on the bridges nearby. What happened next is a matter of dispute. An angry Soviet note charged that a bomb had landed in the small vessel, exploding and tearing off the side of the *Pereyaslavl-Zalesskiy*.

The American reply to the note was abject. Although we did not have enough information to form a judgment on whether the United States had, in fact, damaged the Soviet vessel, said the State Department reply, it was certainly not the intention of the United States to interfere with non-belligerent shipping.

Although the facts will probably never be discovered completely, the case presents some extraordinary aspects. For one thing, even the Soviets charged that only *one* bomb had damaged their shipping, and that it had fallen in the small vessel, not on the *Pereyaslavl-Zalesskiy*. Nevertheless, the

Soviet ship, a small four-stacker, had the side rip-
ped off, and the engines completely disabled, so that
the vessel had to be towed to Vladivostok.

Circumstances suggest, therefore, that the damage
was not caused by the bomb alone, but by an explosion set off in the cargo being transferred to the
barge. In other words, one might reasonably suspect that this non-hostile vessel was bringing in
munitions. The Communists rarely ship a whole
cargo consisting solely of munitions. The practice
is to cover them up in the hold with some innocent
but heavy cargo, such as bags of flour. The Soviets
said that the ship was unloading flour. Nevertheless,
we apologized.

Illogical Policy

Our apology to the chief suppliers of our enemy
was the logical result of an illogical policy. Our
official theory is that the Soviets are not our antagonists in Vietnam. Therefore, the theory says, to deny
Soviet ships access to Haiphong harbor would be an
act of "provocation." As a result, in 1967, Soviet
shipping took the lead in supplying North Vietnam.
Statistics show that of 389 ships that docked at
Haiphong in 1967, 185 were Soviet, 95 were Red
Chinese, 31 were from satellite nations, and 78 were
non-communist.

In gross terms, about eight-five percent of the
military supplies which went into North Vietnam
in 1967 were from the Soviet Union and Soviet-bloc
nations. Without these supplies North Vietnam
could not have waged the war. Soviet technicians

installed the most sophisticated anti-aircraft system seen in combat use today against American planes, a system responsible for our increased aircraft losses. Yet our policy held that the Soviet Union was a non-belligerent.

Once again, the American people were confronted with a strange contradiction. On the one hand, the Soviet Union was acknowledged to be the second strongest military power in the world; the threat of Soviet attack had led us to construct the most impressive defenses the world has ever seen. Yet, on the other hand, our policy seems to be based upon the assumption that the Soviets are anxious for peace, and that the former Soviet threat was "mellowing."

We do not label the Soviets as belligerents in Vietnam because our policy refuses to consider or acknowledge the Soviet intention to conquer the whole world and see it ruled under communism. The incident in Haiphong harbor on January 4, 1968, captures the essence of our foreign policy with regard to communism everywhere. We deny communism's militant nature, we ignore its basic threats to Western values, and we apologize for its existence. Our no-win policy applies not only to hot war, but to cold war too.

While our policymakers obviously do not want the Soviets to win, they do not want the United States to win either. They hope for an illusory truce, in which each side is stalemated in war so that both societies will "converge" in peace.

Some pundits claim that the Soviet social order is mellowing. They say that communism has produced much good along with the bad. The real question, however, is: What is the price that communism has extracted from the Soviet peoples?

Bolshevik Revolution

The year 1967 was the 50th anniversary of the Bolshevik Revolution in the Soviet Union. The Bolshevik take-over was more like a hi-jacking than a revolution. The prelude staged by Lenin presaged what was to come. With typical Communist deceit, the word "Bolshevik" means "majority." Within the cadre of revolutionaries, the Leninists as early as 1903 were a small, but tightly organized splinter, dedicated to ruthless violence and power. Their tactics caused a walk-out of the more idealistic socialists; whereupon Lenin's gang seized the leadership of the movement and proclaimed themselves the Bolsheviks, "the majority faction." Lenin's weak opponents meekly accepted the designation of "Mensheviks," the Minority, even though they were numerically superior.

The Bolshevik Revolution itself came eight months after the overthrow of the Czar. A democratic, representative Duma, or Parliament, had been called. The Mensheviks could not believe that the Bolsheviks were as ruthless or as strong as they proclaimed. At this time, the Bolsheviks had only 105 representatives from local soviets as against 248 Mensheviks and 285 so-called Socialist Revolutionaries. The Mensheviks thought that, with the overthrow of the Czar, Lenin was mellowing. Lenin's celebrated arrival from Switzerland was an occasion of rejoicing, for all the revolutionaries thought they could work together for mutual aims. They were stunned by his denunciations of the liberal revolutionary government. When the Bolsheviks, still a highly disciplined minority, seized power through force of arms on November 7, 1917, the Mensheviks lost their position and their own country.

The lesson of the Bolsheviks and the Mensheviks is still with us today. The Menshevik mentality has migrated to our own shores, even though communism has spread its rule from the original 160 million Soviet subjects until it now rules more than thirty-six percent of the earth's population.

International communism, on conservative estimates, has been responsible for some 83 million deaths since the coup of 1917. At least 45 million of these have been in the Soviet Union itself. Stalin boasted that the man-made famines of 1932–1933 killed 10 million peasants who were refusing to give up their land. Those who listen to communist propagandists today forget that before the revolution 71 percent of the cultivated lands were in small holdings of 135 acres or less. Before the revolution, peasants owned 82 percent of the cattle, 86 percent of the horses, and produced a grain surplus for export. For the period 1906–1913, Russia's industrial growth rate exceeded the rate in the same period for the United States, Great Britain, or Germany. In less than a decade, before the revolution, production had doubled. Russia was second only to the United States in railroad mileage. Russia had more universities than England, France, and Germany, with one-third of the students attending on scholarship. Although Czarist terror seemed formidable at the time, only 32,000 convicts were at hard labor at the peak, and the death penalty was outlawed except for cases of political assassination.

Communist Achievements

After 50 years of communism in the Soviet Union, the Soviet gross national product (GNP) was only forty-five percent of that of the United States, $333 billion as against $739 billion. Of the major industrial nations, the USSR was fifth in GNP. In per capita income, the USSR was thirteenth; and in overall social and economic services, twentieth. The average weekly earnings for a worker in 1965–1966 was $26, with millions subsisting on the so-called legal minimum of $10 per week. Food took 60 percent of a worker's earnings in the USSR, as against 19 percent in the United States. But the most telling statistic of all was that 50 percent of wage earners in the Soviet Union were women—proof that a man could not support a family with his pay check alone.

The human costs have been staggering. Hardly any family was not touched by arrests for slave labor—a fact which leads us to believe that over fifty million people have served in the slave labor camps. Even after fifty years, refugee information indicates that one million were still held. One camp, only 250 miles from Moscow, still held 70,000 in the fiftieth anniversary year.

In 1967, the Soviet regime celebrated fifty years of personal terror, with neighbor spying upon neighbor, husband upon wife, and son upon father. The neighborhood organized spy corps still numbered six million. There were 6,000 local schools to train disseminators of domestic propaganda—propaganda aimed entirely at Soviet citizens. On a higher level, 177 regional institutes gave advanced propaganda training. The Stalin constitution was still in effect. The Supreme Soviet—that is, the supposed national legislature—was still meeting only for a few days each year to rubber-stamp decisions handed down by the Communist Party.

Although indications were that the open terror had abated somewhat, it was clear that the totalitarian nature of the regime made any significant liberalization improbable. The KGB—the secret police—carried on as before, and was known to take over when local police allowed disturbances to get out of hand. Recent reorganizations in the Soviet leadership brought the KGB directly into the policy-making control of the Central Committee of the Communist Party. As Svetlana Stalin pointed out, many of her father's henchmen (from Brezhnev on down) participated in directing the blood purges and were still sitting on the Central Committee. Miss Stalin maintains that deteriorating conditions were a reason for her defection.

How could a system so brutal and inefficient survive without collapsing, much less expand to such a strength in fifty years? Communism has never collapsed because the West has never interfered with its growth. In fact, the West's policy has been exactly the opposite. Despite tactical challenges, the underlying strategy of the West witlessly has served to strengthen the hands of the Communists.

United States Policy

The fashionable experts divide the United States policy toward the Soviet Union into the Stalin Era, the Cold War Era, and the Age of Detente. United States policy is supposed to have moved from a period of cooperation with a grand ally during

World War II, to the supposed militant "anti-communism" of the policy of containment, down to the
present time, when an era of mutual trust and confidence is to gradually establish itself, despite such
temporary set-backs as the Cuban missile crisis and
the Vietnam war.

The cold reality is somewhat different:

1. Our official "anti-communism" has been
mere rhetoric; our policies, rarely successful,
have been directed at the alleged nationalist
expansionism of the Soviet Union itself, not at
the international conspiracy controlled from
Moscow.

2. Our basic attitudes have remained unchanged since the Stalin Era.

These two facts will become much clearer if we
discard the shallow image-making of the mass news
media. Instead, the place to look for a true understanding of our policies is in the major negotiations
we have conducted with the Communists. Here, the
meaning and direction of our policies is distilled to
its quintessence. All the talk, all the rhetoric, all the
headline-grabbing actions evaporate over the hard
wood of the conference table. At such moments, the
world learns what United States policy actually
seeks.

Yalta

The essence of today's policy toward Red China
is unchanged from the spirit of Yalta. The present
fate of the Communist satellite nations in Eastern
Europe was firmly established at Potsdam. The

exact outlines of the Vietnam War were spelled out in the indeterminate negotiations at Panmunjom.

One need only to compare the Soviet aims with stated United States policies at these conferences to understand why communism has been advancing while the free world has been withdrawing. The working papers and briefing books used at Yalta, now published as official government documents, show clearly that the assumptions of American policy in the Far East were stated in such a way as to put forward exactly what the Soviets were seeking to obtain.

At Yalta, a major Soviet goal, and one which Stalin mentioned over and over again, was to secure concessions in Manchuria, particularly with regard to railroads and ports; United States policy was to force China to give concessions, or—as expressed in the famous top-secret agreement that was kept under wraps for a whole year—"The President will take measures to obtain . . . concurrence."

The Soviets, of course, were anxious to help their Chinese comrades at Yenan; United States policy was to help the Chinese Communists at Yenan. The Soviets maintained that Mao's revolution was the only true revolution in Asia; the United States maintained that Chiang Kai-shek's domain on the mainland of China was being weakened by dissident elements and widespread popular discontent, while Communist China was growing in material and popular strength.

In short, Soviet policy declared that Chiang Kai-shek's government was decadent and corrupt, and that the Chinese people welcomed change. United States policy declared that Chiang's government was decadent and corrupt, and that the Chinese people welcomed change. The Soviet goal was to force Chiang Kai-shek to accept a united front government that would have Communists in positions of power; the continuing American policy was to force Chiang Kai-shek to accept a united front government that was to be "broadly representative" of all factions.

Molotov told U.S. Ambassador Patrick J. Hurley that the Chinese Communists were "not true Communists," and that the Soviet Union was not supporting them. American policy accepted this declaration at face value, proclaiming that the Chinese Communists were just agrarian reformers, true nationalists, who were not part of the international communist conspiracy.

The essence of our posture in the Far East was stated in one of the official State Department briefing books: "The Russians primarily want a China friendly to all its neighbors." In a parallel document, it was again stated succinctly: "We regard Sino-Soviet cooperation as a *sine qua non* of peace and security in the Far East and seek to aid in removing the existing mistrust between China and the Soviet Union and in bringing about close and friendly relations between them."

Interestingly enough, our policy today is identical, despite all the changes which have swept over the Far East. We hold today that Sino-Soviet mistrust is the basic cause of instability in the world; we hold that the threat from Red China comes not from its communism, but from its militant "nationalism."

Between Yalta and the present, our China policy has taken on various appearances, yet at heart nothing has changed. The common denominator of every pronouncement, every action, is the passive acceptance of Communist rule. These actions show we are opposed to Communist aggression but not to communism. We oppose militancy, but not bloodless subversion. If communism seizes a country by violence, more often than not we step aside lest the violence escalate. Once a country has been seized by whatever means, we are opposed to liberation if liberation demands violent means. Thus our policy of "isolating Red China" by refusing trade and diplomatic recognition is not by itself "anti-Communist." What this policy has done is to isolate Red China militarily from the Chinese on Taiwan who wanted to free her. The U.S. Seventh Fleet patrolling the Formosan Straits has been an effective guarantee that Mao's regime will be left alone to consolidate its power.

United States Subversion

Unmistakable evidence published by the Senate Internal Security Subcommittee in 1952 showed unequivocally that American policy toward China in the Forties was strongly influenced by communist propaganda and agents working with the U.S. State Department and the U.S. Treasury. The chosen instrument was the then prestigious Institute of Pacific Relations. The Senate report said:

> A group of persons operating within and about the Institute of Pacific Relations exerted a substantial influence on United States Far Eastern policy.
>
> A group of persons associated with the IPR attempted, between 1941 and 1945, to change United States policy so as to accommodate

Communist ends and to set the stage for a major United States policy change, favorable to Soviet interests, in 1945.

During the period 1945–49, persons associated with the Institute of Pacific Relations were instrumental in keeping United States policy on a course favorable to Communist objectives in China.

Yet these findings alone do not account for our foreign policy generally. Soviet and American policy is not, and has not been, identical. The difference is that the Soviets actively pursue their own interests, compromising only when necessary to give a foothold for another assault. United States policy refuses to believe that the Soviets have ulterior motives, and declines to challenge Soviet demands. United States and Soviet goals may be divergent, but United States policy has served as the *complement* of the Soviet plan. Our idea of negotiation is to set forth as our goal the very thing that the Soviets desperately want.

Potsdam

The fate of Eastern Europe was carved up at Potsdam, but the technique was the same as at Yalta. At Potsdam, the Soviets sought to have Communist governments recognized in Poland, Hungary, Rumania, and Bulgaria. Even though U.S. intelligence recognized that all anti-communist elements had been excluded from the governments of these countries, we eventually conceded everything that Stalin asked. Our official policy was so weak that we easily accepted Stalin's assurances. The briefing book which our diplomats carried to Potsdam set up the mechanism which enabled us to rationalize that we had been firm. The policy was as follows:

> Whether the desired reorganization of the Governments is brought about by Allied consultation and agreement on an interim regime which would then conduct elections, or by the holding of elections, with adequate guarantees that they would be free, under the present governments, probably would be immaterial. Under the first alternative we might be willing to establish diplomatic relations and conclude peace before the elections; under the second we would wish to postpone this step until after new governments were formed on the basis of the elections. In either case, should it be decided that Allied observation or supervision of elections was necessary as a means of assuring the freest possible choice on the part of the people, we should be willing to assign our quota of observers. It might be that the elections would be "rigged" anyway, but we would at least have the reports of our own observers on which to base subsequent decisions.

As is usually the case, our protests were weak and ineffectual; we ignored the complaints of our own Allied Control Commissions. The communist governments remained in power.

Once the communist governments were firmly established, our policy changed to one of "containment." The tactic was to "contain" communism within its then-existing borders. Containment was actually a policy of non-interference. The communist regimes were put behind a wall of safety, which gave them time to consolidate their power. Political opponents were liquidated. All those who had some stock in the old order of things—the so-called bourgeoisie—were stripped of their status, and terrorized. The rising generation was indoctrinated in Marxism and atheism. When absolute power had been established from top to bottom, many of these countries could afford to put the terror apparatus out of sight—out of sight, but not out of mind. Communism, we were told, was "mellowing."

The Hungarian uprising of 1956 demonstrated what happens when those under a communist regime take the talk of mellowing seriously. It also demonstrated how well Western inaction is complemented by Soviet action. Learning more from their experience in Hungary, the Soviets adopted a most sophisticated system of control, allowing satellites to take a more independent-sounding line expounded by Soviet-trained native rulers. In actuality, control is maintained through the Communist Party apparatus—the Central Committee of the Soviet Union and its corresponding Central Committees in each communist-dominated country.

Thus on September 7, 1967, the Soviet Union and Hungary signed a Treaty of Friendship, Cooperation, and Mutual Assistance with the Soviet Union. Under this agreement, Hungary pledged itself to remain a Soviet satellite for another twenty years.

There are some who believe that the word "satellite" is outmoded when describing the Soviet empire. The Treaty of September 7, 1967, banished any such beliefs. The Treaty proved that Hungary is completely integrated politically and economically with the Soviet Union. Moscow treats Hungary as a conquered nation, which must pay tribute to its masters. The terms are so humiliating, and so disadvantageous to Hungary, that it is difficult to imagine that the communist bosses would want it publicized. Yet the text was published in full in the official newspaper of the Hungarian Socialist Worker's (Communist) Party the day after it was signed.

The new Treaty consists of nine articles. It replaced a similar Treaty signed in 1948 and retained all important elements of the earlier agreement, but incorporated new provisions to bring it in line with present Soviet foreign policy. It emphasized the "eternal friendship" of the two countries "based on the firm principle of socialist internationalism," and promised bilateral and multilateral economic, scientific, and technical cooperation in accordance with the principles of the "international socialist sharing of the workload" within the so called COMECON—the Communist "Common Market." Hungary's participation in COMECON activities, therefore, became a subject of bilateral state relations between the USSR and Hungary.

The Treaty was regarded by an editorial in the official Hungarian Communist paper as ". . . not only one important factor of our foreign policy, but also an unalterable obligation belonging to the basic pillars of our socialist national existence which serves our best national interests as well as the cause of general peace and the worldwide progress of socialism." Such a candid admission of the fact that the existence of the present regime is dependent on the Soviet Union was one of the rare slips of the

1958: William A. Wieland (right), the U. S. State Department's Cuban expert, never told his superiors that his friend Fidel Castro (left) was a Communist, despite scores of intelligence reports showing Castro's Red connections. Wieland was appointed to his post without proper security procedures, according to the Senate Internal Security Subcommittee.

UPI Radiophoto

Official Communist North Korean photo released January 26, 1968, shows officers and men of the captured U.S.S. Pueblo, seized by the communists on January 23rd.

1968: Because of the heavy flow of gold from the United States Assay Office on Wall Street, bars of gold representing foreign assets are piled on the floor of the vault of the Federal Reserve Bank in New York. UPI Photo

Danny Escobedo, whose 1960 murder conviction was overturned by the U. S. Supreme Court in a landmark decision in 1964, sits in a Chicago police station November 3, 1966, where he was charged with the burglary of a hotdog stand. Police said he was found hiding under a porch after being chased by officers. In 1968, Escobedo was sentenced to 22 years in prison on yet another charge.

U. S. Vice President Lyndon B. Johnson addresses a huge crowd of West Berliners from the balcony of Berlin's Schoeneberg townhall August 19, 1961, telling them that the U. S. would defend its rights only in West Berlin. Four days later East Germany sealed the Berlin wall.

UPI Photo

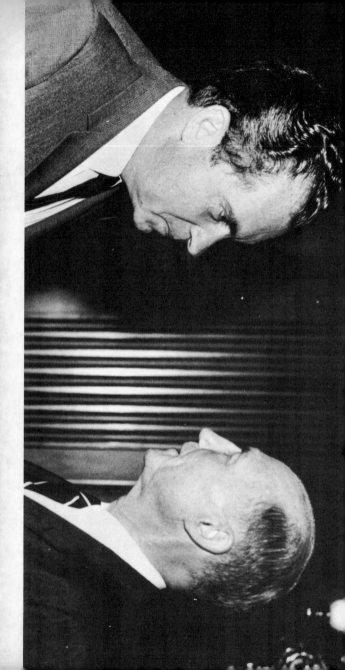

Former Vice President Richard Nixon meets Senator Thurmond at Nation's Capitol.

Ranking members of the Senate Armed Services Committee are from left to right: Senator Stennis, Senator Russell, Senator Margaret Chase Smith, and Senator Thurmond.

Senators Dirksen, Murphy and Thurmond discuss strategy with Governor Ronald Reagan.

tongue printed in an official publication of the Communist Government of Hungary.

The Chairman of the Hungarian Council of Ministers, Jeno Fock, in his speech after the signing of the Treaty, said that ". . . our goals and principles are mutual, our parties and governments profess in the most important matters similar views and act in unity."

Janos Kadar, the head of the Hungarian Communist Party, expressed his thanks to the Soviet Union for the "internationalist" help extended in 1956 to crush the Revolution and he promised the full cooperation of the Government of Hungary with the Soviet Union.

Leonid Brezhnev, the leader of the Soviet Communist Party, lauded Kadar and the Communist Party of Hungary for their contribution to the common cause of revolution.

In 1966, one-third of the entire foreign trade of Hungary was transacted with the Soviet Union. This in itself would be a very dangerous proportion for any country's economy. However, since Hungary in the past two decades was industrialized with emphasis on heavy industry—on instructions from the Kremlin—without having either the raw material basis or the necessary energy sources, an analysis of Hungary's imports from the Soviet Union quickly shows that the entire Hungarian economy can be brought to a standstill if the leaders of the Soviet Union decide to suspend the raw material and energy shipments.

According to the statistics published by the Communists themselves, 67.8 percent of all Soviet imports into Hungary in 1966 consisted of raw materials and semi-finished goods, and 27.5 percent was machinery and factory equipment. If the percentage of the Soviet shipments is compared with the total imports of certain goods, the results are even more startling.

During that period, the Soviet Union supplied to Hungary 85.1 percent of crude oil, 76.8 percent of electric energy, 49.5 percent of cotton, 50.1 percent of coke, 62.7 percent of newsprint, 79.1 percent of lumber, 42.1 percent of rolled steel, and 97.5 percent of pig iron.

There is hardly a worker in Hungary who does not depend for his existence upon raw materials or energy coming from the USSR.

The Hungarian exports to the Soviet Union show similar disproportions. Some 47.3 percent of the shipments to the Soviets consist of machinery and factory equipment, and 29 percent of industrial consumer goods.

Hungary exports to the Soviets more than half of the production of its entire machine and fine mechanical industry, and two-thirds of the total production of the Hungarian pharmaceutical industry.

Hungary's bauxite mining is foremost in Europe, but the bauxite is shipped to the Soviets for smelting, and the aluminum is sold—at a price much higher than the world market would justify—to Hungary for domestic needs. Yet it is well-known that the Soviets sell aluminum cheaply to Poland to make aircraft for the war machine.

In addition to these inequities, Hungary had to join the COMECON which controls the economies of its members. The official communiqué of the Executive Committee of this organization was issued July 8, 1967, and it announced that the economic plans of the member states for the years 1971-1975 must be completely coordinated. This coordination must extend to the international specialization of production, matters of cooperation and standardization, bringing into harmony the building of industrial establishments, geological explorations, scientific and technical cooperation, and matters of furthering the development of mutual trade. The Chairman of the Executive Committee of the COMECON is the representative of the Soviet Union. No further comment is necessary.

Berlin Wall

The Hungarian uprising marked a kind of watershed for the people of Hungary. But for the people of East Germany, the crucial hour was *The Wall*. Recent studies report that the erection of the Wall had a profound effect upon the population. Despite the great attention given to the heroic escapees, the majority of the people of East Germany have turned to passive acceptance of the Communist regime. The Wall was a wall blocking out hope.

The strategy involved in building the Wall was a typical Communist operation. Under the occupation agreements, the Allies had unlimited legal access to East Berlin. Khrushchev wanted to break the agreement and drive the Allies out.

As early as August, 1960, American intelligence reported that the Communist bosses were discussing the feasibility of building a physical wall. Walter Ulbricht, first secretary of the East German Communist Party, urged more caution than Khrushchev; Ulbricht was convinced that East Germany would suffer retaliation if a wall was built.

The plan was to carry out the operation in two stages. In the first stage, the physical wall would be built, but the Allies would be allowed to come and go as before. If this move, in itself illegal, brought no reaction, then in the second stage the Wall itself would be sealed.

As early as April or May of 1961, United States intelligence officers in Berlin learned that the Communist authorities were restricting travel of their own citizens along the East-West border. On August 12–13, the Wall itself was built.

The Wall as a barrier was meaningless at this point. But under all the agreements at Potsdam and thereafter, the occupied zones of Berlin were to be administered jointly. All Allies were to have free access to the other zones. The territories were not to be divided. The Wall's construction was an act of symbolic aggression, since the Communists undertook the job without legal authority. It was concrete evidence of the de facto situation which the Soviets had created. In short, it was a clear test of our will to resist aggression.

The clearest way for the Allies to have asserted their rights would have been immediately to tear down the Wall.

However, if the United States had countered with quick economic sanctions against East Berlin, travel restrictions on Communists, or even quick diplomatic pressure, the Communists would have backed down. In fact, they were prepared to back down if necessary; that was why, at Ulbricht's insistence, the operation was cautiously split in two.

On August 18, 1961, Vice-President Lyndon Johnson arrived in Berlin and made several speeches, all with the same theme: We would defend the rights of *West* Berlin. In effect, we were surrendering our own rights in East Berlin under the written accords. Khrushchev saw that we had no intention of defending our own rights; on August 23, one day after Johnson left Berlin, the Wall was sealed.

Korea

At Berlin, the United States was psychologically disarmed. All the power of our military might is useless, unless we have the will to use it. The war in Vietnam resulted from the indecisive outcome of the war in Korea. From the very beginning, our Vietnam policy was crippled by the long-range policy objectives formulated in Korea. The basic problem in both countries is remarkably the same: An Asian country divided between North and South into communist and free zones; the unacknowledged participation of the Soviet Union; the fear of "escalation" and Red Chinese involvement; restricted targeting and privileged sanctuaries; bloody fighting, but inconclusive results.

The interminable negotiations at Panmunjom spelled out our real policy in Korea. Point by point, the disastrous effect of United States policy was to supply the circumstances that were needed for Soviet policy to accomplish its ends.

The Communists maintained that the Korean War was a just war initiated by the Korean people, with no assistance from the Soviets. The United States policy held that there was no reliable intelligence on Soviet involvement. Throughout the intelligence community, this position was derisively called the Fig Leaf Policy, since positive evidence of Soviet involvement was plentiful. It is interesting that exactly the same procedure was followed in the months leading up to the Cuban missile crisis; it is the same kind of policy we are now following with regard to the Soviet missiles in Cuba.

At Panmunjom, the USSR grandly "took the initiative" in bringing about peaceful settlement of the war. Actually, the Korean operation was inconclusive on both sides. The United States policy was to accept the Soviet initiative in the interest of peace.

The Communist policy was that the Chinese Communist troops swarming across the border were "volunteers." The United States policy dignified the assertion by agreeing to the term "volunteers" at the signing of the peace.

In February, 1950, the Red Chinese and the Soviets signed a mutual defense treaty, which committed the Soviets to assist the Chinese. Despite the fact, therefore, that the Soviets had already taken sides, the United States policy said that we must not bomb Manchuria or the Yalu River bridges since such actions might initiate Soviet intervention.

In the same way, the Communist policy was to secure a lopsided inspection team which included Czechs and Poles. Our policy was to agree to an inspection team which included Czechs and Poles. On another crucial point, the Soviet policy was to hold out for only five ports of entry on either side of divided Korea; the American policy was to accept this demand, even though United States intelligence had originally proposed fourteen ports of entry as the minimum.

In short, the overriding aim of the Communists at Panmunjom was to secure a status quo agreement, that is, a divided Korea. In effect, it meant that the

Communists would regain much of the territory that they had lost, and prevent further losses. The United States policy was to agree to the demilitarized zone which divides Korea today, and still holds down 50,000 U.S. troops today.

The unfinished business in Korea—our no-win war—is ultimately responsible for tempting the Communists to begin the Vietnam conflict. At Panmunjom, the Communists learned that they took no risk. If they won on the battlefield, they won; if they lost on the battlefield, they could go to the conference table and start all over. For the Communists, peace negotiations are nothing but war by a different method.

Sophisticated Soviet Policy

Soviet policy is tailor-made to take advantage of the astounding weaknesses that characterize our official attitude toward communism. The chief weakness is our refusal to acknowledge the increased sophistication and skill evident in Soviet diplomacy. The basic foundation of that diplomacy is this: The foreign policy of the USSR must not be identified with the organized world communist movement under Soviet domination.

During the past decade, United States policy has held that there is no evidence of Soviet control of an international communist conspiracy. Our policymakers have declared over and over again that the Soviet empire is fragmenting. They argue that the United States should support independent communist governments wherever they show signs of manifesting themselves.

No communist government in the world is a

"government" in the Western sense. What we usually refer to as the "government" in these countries is an administrative bureaucracy for executing the decisions of each country's Central Committee of the Communist Party. These governments are no more true governments than the Communist Party of the United States is a political party. They are front operations set up to deal with the captive peoples and with other nations. In each case, the Central Committees consist of hard-core communists under the rigid discipline of Moscow. The communist world does not consider free world governments or their agreements to have any legitimacy. Thus the American policy of pretending that these governments are "independent" complements the Soviet policy line of avoiding identifications of the USSR with a world movement.

Despite assertions that Soviet society is "mellowing," the Soviets continue to say that there is no force in the world that can halt the advance of Soviet society. They say that their cause is invincible. They reassert that the cause of world communism must yield neither to provocation nor to intimidation.

American policy, on the other hand, says that we must not provoke the Soviets since it might increase the danger of general war. The so-called evolutionary processes are said to be bringing about changes within Communist society. Even though the Soviets constantly reiterate their desire to work toward a World Union of Soviet Socialist Republics, uniting the whole of mankind under the hegemony of the international proletariat, our official policy says that no direct reference should be made to the Soviet aim of world domination.

Chapter VI

INTERNAL SECURITY AND UNITED STATES POLICY

Soviet policy not only seeks to advance its aims throughout the world at our expense, but it also seeks to advance its aims within the United States itself. The only obstacle to Soviet expansionism today is the power of the United States; the Soviet aim is to keep that power from being used.

Thus the Soviet policy has been to make disarmament negotiations a vehicle for agitation and for recruiting sympathizers for the Soviet Union, as cast in the guise of the champion of peace and socialism. The pure propaganda of its disarmament posture has been matched by subversive infiltration and direction of pacifist movements in this country. This hard-headed view of disarmament negotiations finds an easy mark in the American policy that we should try to arrive at some form of disarmament in the interests of peace, even to the point of unilateral disarmament on our part.

Soviet policy strove for ratification of the atmospheric nuclear test ban treaty once the 1962 Soviet tests were completed. Despite the fact that the United States did not possess adequate information about the electro-magnetic effects of nuclear explosions in the atmosphere and beyond, the United

States policy was to strive for ratification of the treaty in the Senate.

When both nations are seeking to implement the same policy, the advantages are not always mutual. Both the United States and the Soviet Union sought to have the U.S. Senate ratify the Consular Convention in 1967 to increase the number of consulates and the number of immunities to be enjoyed by nationals posted to those consulates. In a closed society, consuls and their staffs have few opportunities for espionage because of surveillance and restrictions. In an open society, diplomatic immunities are worth far more. Soviet intelligence defectors often relate that ninety percent of their work is gathering technical data from open sources. One ex-spy remarked that he often obtained for free, material he would have paid $50,000 to get through a clandestine operation.

The Soviet Union will have gained far more from this treaty when it chooses to exercise its option. On the floor of the Senate, the prediction was made that the Soviet Presidium would very well embarrass us by refusing ratification, which is for them a purely ceremonial gesture. More than one year after Senate ratification, the Presidium still had not acted.

More recently, the Soviets sought to obtain a treaty on the peaceful uses of outer space in order to keep the United States from placing in orbit, objects carrying nuclear weapons. This policy was a sudden turn-about, which came after extensive Soviet testing of orbital vehicles. The change in circumstances was completely ignored by United States policymakers who had long sought such a treaty. Not long afterward, Soviet development of the Fractional Orbital weapon and the so-called MIRV-type warhead (a multiple warhead capable of hitting individual targets) made it highly likely that the Soviets could violate the outer space treaty without warning—for indeed, the treaty contained no inspection procedures. United States policy continued to hold that orbital or suborbital space weapons would be inefficient.

American policy as a whole betrays an inadequate understanding of the nature of communism and its goals. It is not merely that the policies are wrong, or ill-suited to the attainment of the desired goals; the problem is that the policymakers have had a fundamental change in attitude toward the enemy who is seeking to destroy us.

The Otepka Case

Four years of inquiry by the Senate Internal Security Subcommittee (SISS) into State Department Security practices revealed that the lack of concern for the security of this nation was embodied even in the lack of concern for the security of the State Department itself. The subcommittee report on these hearings raised two paramount issues, growing out of the cooperation of the State Department's career security officer, Otto Otepka, with the subcommittee's investigations.

The first is whether a government employee loyal to his country can, in the line of duty, furnish information confidentially to the appropriate congressional committees when he sees wrongdoing. Congress has a basic right to receive such information, not only for the purpose of formulating new legislation but for reviewing existing programs.

This right has been embodied in a statute, namely, United States Code, Title 5, Section 652(d):

> The right of persons employed in the civil services of the United States, either individually or collectively, to petition Congress, or any Member thereof, or to furnish information to either House of Congress or to any Committee or Member thereof, shall not be denied or interfered with. (As amended June 10, 1948, c. 447, 62 Stat. 354; 1949 Reorganization Plan No. 5, effective August 19, 1949, 14 F.R. 5227, 63 Stat. 1067.)

The State Department's position has been variously, (1) that no wrongdoing may be disclosed unless the disclosure is authorized presumably by the wrongdoers; (2) that information from personnel files may not be disclosed in any case; (3) that any paper may be protected by calling it an official paper. Any of these interpretations is manifestly contrary to the plain meaning of the statute, yet the State Department has found no extenuating circumstances for Otepka's action in cooperating with the subcommittee.

An agency that had nothing to hide would be anxious for an employee to make use of this right. One would think that such an agency would be looking for extenuating circumstances if an employee had failed to do his duty toward Congress.

As a matter of fact, Otepka furnished no substantive matter from personnel files that was not already a matter of subcommittee or public record. Otepka furnished copies of the document only to illustrate security procedures and to prove that his superior had lied under oath to this subcommittee concerning security procedures.

The second issue, therefore, concerns what the Department of State had to hide. As is amply set forth in the report and in the preceding volumes of testimony, the State Department was trying to hide a new policy of phasing out effective security procedures. The highest officers of the State Department no longer believed in the mandate to maintain critical standards of suitability and loyalty in employing personnel. Quite simply Otepka and a small band of associates were in the way.

This attitude was amply documented in the report on State Department security practices as follows:

1. Officers with little or no experience in security evaluation were placed in positions making evaluation policy.

2. The functions of the Office of Security were dismantled piecemeal, and its staff transferred out.

3. The specialized personnel security files were broken up.

4. Otepka was criticized for being "too thorough" in a job where it is impossible to be too thorough.

5. A "personnel panel" with no written guidelines assumed many of the security evaluation functions.

Many other moves are covered more fully in the report, but these steps show clearly the new policy. Since the loyalty of Otepka and his associates stood in the way of that policy, the Department began to move directly against him.

1. He was assigned to attend the National War College, in order to remove him from his duties.

2. He was detailed on make-work projects for the same reasons.

3. After his testimony before the Internal Security Subcommittee, he was publicly humiliated, removed from his offices, deprived of his papers and safe. His telephone was bugged, his trashbag searched, and carbons from his typewriter examined.

4. His loyal associates were transferred away from their duties to a make-work project where they had no contact with other State Department employees.

As the situation evolved, the State Department began, finally, to move against the subcommittee itself, in that:

1. Unusual delays were experienced in summoning witnesses and in official correspondence.

2. Witnesses arrived with instructions to limit their testimony and to refuse to discuss certain vital areas.

3. The "third agency rule" of not revealing material supplied by another government unit was given an extreme interpretation which blocked information on many matters.

4. In news releases and public correspondence, the State Department indulged widely in half-truths and quoting out of context.

5. Three State Department officers lied to the subcommittee, and were later forced to recant when the question of perjury became a matter of discussion on the Senate floor.

Perhaps the most illustrative example of the State Department attitude came when John F. Reilly, head of the Office of Security, testified that the reason why he had told half-truths was because the subcommittee had not asked him the right questions. Ironically, one of the original State Department charges against Otepka was that he had furnished the subcommittee with a list of the right questions.

State Department personnel security policy was manifestly contrary to the intentions of Congress. State Department officers deliberately attempted to hide this fact from an agency of Congress charged with overseeing security practices. The State Department indulged in illegal acts, the destruction of the careers of honest men, misrepresentation, and perhaps perjury, in order to prevent Congress from carrying out its constitutional functions.

Walt Whitman Rostow

Otepka first ran into trouble in 1960 when he expressed reservations about a proposed clearance for Walt Whitman Rostow. Three times before, according to the brief Otepka filed before a State Department hearing examiner, Rostow had been denied a State Department clearance under the Eisenhower Administration to handle sensitive data, and Otepka indicated to Dean Rusk and Attorney General Designate Robert Kennedy that he would probably still evaluate Rostow's file in the same manner.

This episode had a decidely different effect on the careers of the two principals involved. Rostow was given immediate clearance as a White House aide, where the only security criterion is the President's say-so; he moved under this clearance to the State Department Policy Planning Council, and later became, ironically, Special Assistant to the President for National Security Affairs. Otepka became the victim of a scheme which involved perjury, wire tapping, and character assassination, in an effort to remove him from his important post.

On the other hand, Rostow has taken such a great hand in shaping United States policy that he can be said almost to be the official·spokesman for the President. On February 23, 1967, Rostow made a full-dress speech at Leeds University, England, on what he called "The Great Transition." In this speech may be seen the deepest motivations of United States policy.

For Rostow, the cold war is over. He said at Leeds that "the struggle in Vietnam might be the last great confrontation of the postwar era." He looked forward to "reconciliation and cooperation with respect to endemic disputes arising either with Communist regimes or between non-Communist states." He told his audience that this generation will move "towards a liquidation of the key issues of the Cold War in Europe, and towards arms control, while working to bring a more moderate Communist China into a normal relationship to Asia and the world."

Such thoughts as these could not be better calculated to develop complacency toward communism, despite Rostow's frequently reiterated "anti-communism." Rostow said at Leeds that the Soviet concept of "wars of national liberation" was old-fashioned; he believed that the Soviet policy was to create an atmosphere of settlement, reconciliation and cooperation. He said this even while "wars of national liberation," such as in Vietnam, were being supported in two hemispheres.

Rostow went on to say that in the interest of peace and international cooperation, we must trade with communist countries and make the most of the forces of moderation which have emerged in the USSR and Eastern Europe since 1953. This just happens to fit in with the Soviet policy of obtaining concessions from the United States in East-West trade in order to overcome heavy industry shortages.

In the same way, Rostow said that we must bring Mainland China into a normal relation to the world community. On the other hand, the announced Soviet policy is identical—to bring Mainland China into a normal relation to the world community. Indeed, Rostow says that the aggressive, romantic revolutionaries are passing from the scene, while aggressive impulses have diminished in the technologically mature Soviet Union.

The Soviet policy puts it a little differently: The Soviets say that the rash and crude tactics of the Chinese Communists are so counter-productive that it would take at least 200 years to establish world communism. The Soviets' aim is more sophisticated: They want to do it in twenty years.

William A. Wieland

The Soviets' boast may be measured against their successes. One need look no further than Cuba to see how catastrophic American failures were set in motion by false concepts of policy within the State Department. The nerve center of information concerning pre-Castro Cuba was the State Department's Caribbean desk. In charge of the desk was one William A. Wieland.

The Wieland case brought about the first confrontation between Otepka and his superiors. In August, 1961, Otepka completed an extensive summary and analysis of various charges against Wieland, including the allegation that Wieland was the recipient of significant intelligence information indicating that Fidel Castro was a Communist, but that he, Wieland, had concealed that information. The summary was important enough for Otepka to recommend that the Foreign Service should determine whether Wieland had been guilty of misconduct.

Shortly thereafter, Otepka's superiors orally instructed him to issue a security clearance to Wieland, even though regulations required a written determination of Wieland's security status before the clearance could be issued. Otepka's refusal to break the regulations resulted in a sudden decision by the Department of State to reduce the size of the work force in the Office of Security because of "reduced appropriations." Otepka was to be reassigned to other duties.

In January 1962, a newspaper reporter questioned President Kennedy about Wieland, whom the reporter described as a security risk. The question was challenged by the President. Immediately thereafter, Otepka was instructed in writing to issue a security clearance for Wieland. Regardless of his own evaluation of the case, Otepka was required to issue the clearance. He did so.

However, in February 1962, Otepka developed new evidence indicating that Wieland had made false statements with respect to the number of times he had personally met with Castro. Otepka recommended that the case be reopened, reinvestigated, and readjudicated. His recommendation was ignored.

A few months later, the Senate Internal Security Subcommittee, which had been looking into the

Wieland case, along with other security practices in the State Department, singled out Wieland as an example. The Subcommittee's statement said:

> The case of William Wieland, like the majority of security cases, does not involve loyalty. It involves such factors as integrity and general suitability.
>
> Mr. Wieland should be viewed . . . as an example: His record and conduct and the handling of his security case combine to provide a case history which illustrates much of what is wrong with the State Department from a security standpoint.

The subcommittee did not shrink from pointing out the precise violations of regulations and good sense in the Wieland case:

1. Wieland was appointed to a position at the State Department for which his qualifications were highly doubtful—at a salary more than twice what he was making as a civilian.

2. Wieland was appointed without any security check.

3. Wieland's appointment was effective even before he filled out an application form.

4. Wieland falsified his job application by omission.

5. When Wieland later filled out an expanded personal history form, he falsified that by direct misstatement.

Despite these irregularities, Wieland had a direct hand in shaping our policy with respect to Cuba both before and after Castro's takeover. The report said:

He held a position which by definition made him one of the State Department's experts in Latin American affairs, and Cuban affairs particularly. One of the things the Department paid him for was his expertise—his own judgment based on his own experience. Yet he never told his superiors officially or wrote in any Department paper, down to the very day when Fidel Castro stood before the world as a self-proclaimed Marxist, what he told friends privately as early as 1958—or earlier—that Castro "is a Communist" and "is surrounded by Commies [and] * * * subject to Communist influences."

To Mr. Wieland's desk came, over a period of years, great quantities of intelligence respecting the Communist nature and connections of the Castro movement, of Castro himself and his principal lieutenants. The committee was unable to document a single instance in which Mr. Wieland passed any of this material up to his superiors or mentioned it as credible in any report or policy paper.

Mr. Wieland became an active apologist for Fidel Castro. . . .

As a consequence of the United States decisions in which Wieland was a crucial figure, the Soviets were able to advance their designs almost upon our shores. Further hearings before the Senate Internal Security Subcommittee in the spring of 1967 indicated that the Soviet Union was continuing to maintain Cuba as an armed camp, bristling with missiles which threatened the security of the United States and the peace of the world. The situation recalled warnings issued by alert observers in January, 1962, and which the same subcommittee aired, months before the Administration reluctantly agreed that intelligence experts possessed "hard" evidence of a Soviet buildup.

The delay in acknowledging Soviet penetration of this hemisphere in 1962 brought on the critical confrontation between the United States and the USSR which came to be known as the "missile crisis." By allowing the Soviet buildup in Cuba to continue to significant levels, unimpeded, the Administration lost control of the situation and brought the world to the brink of war.

The result was that the United States had to back down from the explosive tension. The United States, as subsequent events have shown, agreed in effect to guarantee the sanctity of Cuba as a communist bastion in the Caribbean. We did nothing to counteract U Thant's subtle instructions to Castro to refuse international inspection of the missile sites. There has never been any convincing evidence that the Soviet missiles were removed by the Soviet Union. The Cuban confrontation must be regarded as having ended in a Soviet tactical victory.

Between 1962 and 1967, the Soviets solidified that victory and made gains. According to the testimony of sworn witnesses before the Internal Security Subcommittee, Cuba no longer existed as an independent nation. Castro remained as a fiery, but powerless, leader symbolizing the "revolution."

Experts testifying before the subcommittee in 1967 said that Cuba was being run by the Soviet military commanders on the island. The Soviets controlled the economy. They controlled the armed forces and the fleets of so-called "fishing boats."

They trained and exported up to 10,000 guerrillas a year for the encouragement of subversion throughout Latin America.

Cuba itself was described as a rocky fortress. Its natural cave formations were widely interconnected with man-made tunnels and reinforced with concrete. One tunnel was reported to be large enough to transport 100-foot missiles for forty-five miles underground. Missile sites and defense installations were said to be located near the entrances to various tunnels.

Witnesses in 1967 described hidden aircraft hangars, burrowed into the hillside. Ballistic missiles of at least intermediate range were reported as having been moved about under cover of darkness, with whole sections of cities systematically blacked out to obscure the movement. Sophisticated radar and guidance systems were said to have blossomed at strategic locations. A witness told of one underground installation at Camaguey concealed by a chicken farm.

Yet the Administration, deluded by a spirit of "detente" with communism, refused to take these reports seriously. There is a direct connection between the belief that communism is no longer dangerous and the posture that internal security practices no longer need be stringent. The case of William Wieland shows that the opposite is also true: When internal security practices are lax, the opportunity is present for the rise to power of policymakers who see no danger in communism. The price of liberty is eternal vigilance; those who are making the policies designed to protect our liberty, must also believe in vigilance.

Chapter VII

SOCIALIZING THE "THIRD WORLD"

Late in 1967, the United States Government decided to allow this nation to become dependent upon the Soviet Union for its supply of chrome ore. At least, such was the effect of a decision, the implications of which went far beyond the immediate facts of the case. On the surface, the decision in question was merely a minor matter, acted upon pursuant to the Rhodesian embargo.

The facts of the matter were not difficult. The Foote Mineral Company, an American company based in Exton, Pennsylvania, asked for a special import license to bring in a small quantity of chrome ore—also called chromite—from its own mines in Rhodesia. The quantity requested was just enough to keep a caretaker operation going at the mines.

The importation of chromite was embargoed by the President in January, 1967, along with many other significant Rhodesian exports, in support of the worldwide embargo established by the United Nations Security Council against the independent government of Premier Ian Smith. Even then, the only two countries in the world producing significant quantities of metallurgical grade chromite were the Soviet Union and Rhodesia. Presumably, such a policy could only have been a short-range tactic to apply pressure against the Smith government.

Despite the embargo, Rhodesia stood as firm in November, 1967, as she did when she declared independence two years earlier. Most nations in the world found it convenient to ignore or by-pass the embargo when their immediate or profitable interests were threatened. Quantities of Rhodesian chromite were exported to many countries in one way or another.

However, Foote Mineral was trapped by the United States sanctions. Its U.S. refinery had formerly absorbed the total output of its Rhodesian mines. If Foote Mineral bootlegged chromite to foreign producers, it would undercut its own United States operations.

Foote Mineral was spending $900,000 a year just to keep the mines operating on skeleton crews. If mines have to be closed, skilled crews disperse. The mines fill with water. Machinery rusts. Foote estimated that it would take a minimum of three years to reactivate the mines if closed, at a cost of millions of dollars.

Meanwhile, our strategic stockpile of chromite was down to a three-year supply. There is no known substitute for the finished product, chromium, in the production of stainless steels and other sophisticated alloys. The Soviets, aware that the United States embargo had created a communist monopoly, immediately raised prices on new contracts by increases of up to twenty percent.

Under these circumstances, Foote Mineral asked only for permission to import 40,000 tons of chromite—just enough to support caretaker operations at the mines. The American national interest surely demanded that the artificial sanctions be lifted— if not in entirety, then at least as regards chromite. Yet Foote Mineral was asking for a bare minimum of an exception—enough to protect American jobs at home, American investments abroad, and the long-range American national security implications of maintaining a continuous supply of chromite in the free world.

Nevertheless, the State Department said no. The Foreign Assets Control Division of the Treasury Department—the agency charged with enforcement —was prepared to grant the exception, but somewhere at a high policy level in the State Department, the application was turned down.

The application was turned down, despite the danger that the Soviet Union might get a stranglehold on our chromite supply.

The application was turned down, despite the threat to American jobs and investments.

The application was turned down, because Rhodesia was a pro-Western nation.

These three facets of the case require some explanation. The threat of Soviet control of our chromite supply was disregarded by the State Department; in fact, United States officials acknowledged, if not encouraged, the growing dependence upon Soviet sources. Our official policy holds that the Soviet Union is a "responsible" world power that is no longer a threat. The President himself has urged greater trade and closer contacts with the Soviet Union.

In the context of "detente" and "communism is mellowing," the Soviet threat is no threat at all. Therefore, the fact that Soviet chromite is the only alternative to Rhodesian chromite is of little consequence to the way the State Department views things.

Nor is it important in our policy scheme that American jobs or investments might suffer. The relatively small number of those engaged in the chromite industry do not form a powerful bloc in domestic politics. Our policymakers are ready to sacrifice so-called "selfish" interests to new definitions of the national interest.

The now-classic exposition of this attitude appears in Walt Whitman Rostow's book, *The United States in the World Arena* (1960):

> It is a legitimate American national objective to see removed from all nations—including the United States—the right to use substantial military force to pursue their own interests. Since this residual right is the root of national sovereignty and the basis for the existence of an international arena of power, it is therefore an American interest to see *an end to nationhood* as it has been historically defined.

This book was a project of the Center for International Studies, at a time when the Center was admittedly supported preponderantly by funds from the U.S. Central Intelligence Agency. As Rostow himself became more important in the policy councils of the President, the implications of this thesis have spread. Sovereignty and independence are at the heart of Western concepts of the nation, just as individual freedom and the inviolability of the human person are at the heart of the Western idea of Man.

Those who are seeking "an end to nationhood" are seeking an end to manhood as well. They want to redefine freedom, both for the nation and for the citizen. They view the world as divided into three camps: The nations of the West, the nations of the communist camp, and the so-called "third world" of the underdeveloped, neutralist nations. By redefining freedom, they seek a world socialist order in which the communist nations, the formerly sovereign nations of the West, and the nations of the third world lie down under the same socialist yoke.

Building Socialism

The sympathy of our policymakers toward socialism, however, is not mere blindness or ill-conceived policy. The encouragement of socialism has been an important element of the definition of United States interests in the world. It is a policy directed not only toward the rest of the world, but toward United States domestic affairs as well. The development of a world socialist order, in which the United States would simply be another socialist cog, is the overriding policy guiding us throughout the world.

"Mutual accommodation" with the Soviet Union is but one element of the grand plan. The dream of an international world order by definition—the new definition—means the subordination of the United States to a global community. Therefore, our foreign policy contemplates the "mellowing" of communism into non-violent socialism, and the development of underdeveloped areas of the world according to socialist forms of government.

Sophisticated socialists smile whenever they are accused of being socialists. The word seems old-fashioned, doctrinaire, even romantic. Today's socialist prefers to use words like "modernization," "pragmatism," "moderation" to describe their policies. They are flexible. They admit mixtures of public and private control in their enterprises. They allow private capital to profit from international agreements and regulations. They seek to grant concessions, both economic and diplomatic, even while our own soldiers are dying fighting communists in one of our self-induced stalemates.

Nevertheless, their underlying principle is that public decision—decision by those who have seized power within the bureaucracy of our government— is to be preferred to the decisions of private individuals or of their elected representatives. Their rationale is that the common good—as they define it—always supersedes individual will.

The "Creative Elite"

These policies are not acceptable to the mass of the American people, few of whom have reconciled themselves to socialist interference in their own lives or in the policies of their nation. That is why our socialists flatter themselves by imagining that they are a "creative elite," whose international thinking is far advanced over the muddled thinking of the backward American citizen.

Such a position results in a disastrous alienation of the socialist clique—many of whom have fine minds—from American culture, rooted as it is in aspirations spiritual and patriotic.

The notion of a "creative elite" becomes the justification for all kinds of revolutionary action. At every level, the socialists feel that they must attack American society and reconstitute it in a socialist image. Students leave their books behind, and march in the streets for emotions instead of ideas. Professors seek to shape their students' minds by suppressing facts, limiting alternatives and denigrating loyalty to parents, country, and God.

The mass media distort images by selective reporting and subtle insinuations. Worst of all, the bureaucrats in government feel that they are perfectly justified to use the organs and resources of government to remake social patterns, to propagandize for government control, to beat reluctant citizens down by force, and to reward covertly all men who will advance the goals of the "creative elite," even in the face of majority opposition.

Thus it becomes clear why Rhodesia became the particular target of those who have visions of the new world order.

Rhodesia proclaimed itself a pro-Western country at a time when the West has turned against itself. Rhodesia stood up for independence, courage, honor and responsibility, at a time when the dominant trend in the world has been toward collectivism, passivity, compromise, and expediency. Rhodesia's Declaration of Independence was a conscious emulation of America's Declaration of 1776, and the principles for which that Declaration stood.

Despite nearly two centuries' difference, the Rhodesian and American actions were remarkably

similar. Both declared independence of Britain—
without Britain's consent. Both declared independence reluctantly, concluding that the British Sovereign had violated the rights that were theirs by law.
Both declared independence so that their peoples
could re-establish the concept of civil liberty under
law that extended through the centuries back to the
Magna Carta.

Like America, Rhodesia saw itself as a frontier
country, developing itself by its own hard work and
initiative.

Rhodesians praised the virtues of toil, self-educa-
tion, prudence, thrift and love of the land. In the
same manner, they wanted to inculcate the same virtues in the native tribes who lived in the midst of
civilization without yet having the capability of par-
ticipating in civilization. They organized an educational program second only, in all of Africa, to
South Africa. To provide incentive, they offered
every native the power to participate in government
to the degree to which self-improvement was attained. They even made it clear that the natives
could well control the government within a generation, if enough attained the modest requirements.

The Rhodesians looked to America for sympathy
and understanding, conceiving of the American
people as their brothers in the same exhilarating
experience of achieving independence.

They overlooked one thing.

They overlooked the fact that true independence
and stability is out of fashion. To be respectable today, nations must boast of being "interdependent"
instead of independent. They must be linked with
every other nation, not by chains of friendship, but
by webs of international agreements and protocols.

To be respectable, a nation must repudiate foreign investment and private enterprise and drive out foreign technicians. To qualify for foreign aid, a nation must yoke itself to central planning in economics and revert to one-party nationalism in politics. In short, to be called modern, a country must go native.

Anti-Colonialism

United States foreign policy has fallen into the trap of seeking to wipe out "the vestiges of colonialism." Like every other human undertaking, colonialism was a mixture of good and evil. The Thirteen American Colonies would testify to that. Yet whatever the evil our forefathers suffered because of the colonial relationship, colonialism determined the very character and stamp of our nation in a way of which every American can be proud.

So too, colonialism brought exploitive practices and misery to many quarters of the globe; but it also brought government, education, Christianity, and Western technology. Anti-colonialism is rather an essential tenet of Marxist theoreticians, who view the colonial system as a necessary extension of capitalism. The downfall of colonialism is regarded by socialists as an essential preliminary to the fall of capitalism.

Since capitalism is regarded as an unmitigated evil, it is an article of faith among socialists that "the people" are struggling to throw off "their foreign oppressors" just as "the workers" are supposed to be struggling against their capitalist bosses. Any sign of pro-Western sentiment in a former colonial region is therefore suspect. Pro-Westernism is tantamount to pro-capitalism, than which there is no greater shame. Any socialist or crypto-communist who purports to be leading "his people" to "democracy" immediately wins support, even though most of "his people" may never have heard of him.

United States policy backed Sukarno in Indonesia, until "his people" threw him out in a bloody struggle.

United States policy backed Nkrumah in Ghana, until "his people" threw him out.

United States policy backed Ben Bella in Algeria, until "his people" were trapped in a socialist police state, unable to free themselves or even to feed themselves.

United States policy covertly backed Castro in Cuba until Cuba became a Soviet bastion which is only ninety miles from our shores.

United States policy backed Ho Chi Minh until . . .

Sukarno was "the George Washington of Indonesia."

Nkrumah was "the George Washington of Ghana."

Ben Bella was "the George Washington of Algeria."

Castro was "the George Washington of Cuba."

Ho Chi Minh was "the George Washington of Indochina."

Of course, George Washington's people never threw him out.

It is not coincidence that United States policy has so often backed the most vicious and most despicable native leaders simply because they preach socialism and democracy. We have deliberately sought to build socialism throughout the world, even though socialism is basically antagonistic to traditional American practices and beliefs. Our policy has actually been to strengthen leaders who are hostile to us—the so-called neutralists.

Socialism and Communism

Many of our policymakers are convinced that socialism is the wave of the future, and that it is the only alternative to communism. Such a view is rarely presented to the public, although it is a view that dominates the highest policy centers.

In 1962, for example, the public got a glimpse of this reasoning when CBS reporter Eric Sevareid discussed the activities of the CIA with CIA Chief Allen Dulles:

> SEVAREID: There's been a general argument in the Left or liberal press writers in this country . . . that the CIA people have sort of automatically tended to support very extreme Right Wing groups in foreign countries because of an obsession with communism, and have therefore set back progressive democratic possibilities in foreign countries.
>
> DULLES; I think just the opposite is the case . . . I would say that by and large we were quicker than others to recognize the dangers in these situations, because I have often felt in many countries that the strongest antagonists of the Communists, and those who knew them best were often—not always—some of the socialist leaders. (*CBS Reports,* April 26, 1962).

Not always, of course—Sukarno, Nkrumah, Ben

Bella, Castro, Ho Chi Minh. Our "containment" policy was not only containment of communism; it was containment of ourselves, too. Instead of putting forth the American principles of free enterprise, local initiative, divided political responsibilites, we took the position that these principles did not apply anywhere else. We encouraged socialism, made central planning a requirement of our aid, and apologized for one-man-one-rule dictatorial regimes.

Lest there be some suspicion that Allen Dulles and the CIA were promoting their own little policies, subverting the official wishes of the President, it may be well to quote another exchange in the same program:

> SEVAREID: Are you saying, Mr. Dulles, that there have been no cases abroad where the activities of CIA have conflicted with our official State Department foreign policy in those countries?
> DULLES: There have been none.
> SEVAREID: None at all?
> DULLES: None at all.

Nor was Mr. Dulles alone in his opinion. Early in 1967, the scandal of the CIA's supporting the notoriously left-wing organization, the National Student Association, came out into the open. Scores of other organizations collectively received millions of dollars from the public treasury. With but one or two exceptions, the politics of these groups ranged from extremely liberal to doctrinaire socialist. Again, the excuse was put forward that only organizations of this type could be "effective" in combating communism.

Moreover, every statement put out upon that occasion by all those who had been privy to the actions of the CIA directly supported the point that the CIA was merely the agent of those in power. This point was reiterated by Lyndon Johnson, Hubert Humphrey, Robert Kennedy, Nicholas Katzenbach, Walt Whitman Rostow, as well as by the current CIA Chief, Richard Helms. The President and his closest advisers knew at all times what the CIA was doing. The CIA was simply carrying out the official policy of building socialism behind the backs of the American people.

It is a policy which looks with alarm upon Red China crossing the indefinite borders of socialist India, but is silent when India seizes and occupies Goa, the overseas province of our NATO ally, Portugal.

It is a policy which finances Norman Thomas in a program to help Juan Bosch take over Santo Domingo, later to be repudiated by "his people"—but which kidnaps the moderate Brigadier General Elias Wesin y Wesin and spirits him out of his country.

It is a policy which imposes the catastrophically incompetent socialist labor leader, Cyrille Adoula, upon the people of the Congo, while the genuinely popular Moise Tshombe is hounded out of Katanga with United Nations fire and sword because he believes in Christianity, capitalism, and the West.

Rhodesia, therefore, made one mistake when she expected the United States to be pro-Western. Rhodesia did not understand that the leaders of the United States no longer kept faith with the American heritage.

Accordingly, on January 7, 1967, the President of the United States, acting in accord with a resolution passed by the General Assembly of the United

Nations, issued Executive Order No. 11332, forbidding United States businessmen from engaging either in export or import trade with Rhodesia in all the substantial categories of Rhodesian commerce. He issued this order so as to bring Rhodesia to heel, to make it submit to the demands of socialist Britain, and to make Rhodesia get in line with the socialist world order.

Panama Canal

The Rhodesians, perhaps because of their remoteness from world affairs, did not realize that the American lust for socialism had gone so far that the United States was even condemning itself for its own "colonialism" on its own sovereign territory of the Canal Zone.

There are few works which have been more characteristic of the American spirit than the Panama Canal. After the other major nations of the West had failed to construct a canal, American technology, courage, boldness, and determination successfully carried to completion a project of immense conception.

Nor has such a project ever been conducted in a greater spirit of fairness and magnanimity. The project was undertaken as a mandate for civilization— and the United States has never departed from that responsibility. The Canal has always been open to all comers, on an equal basis, for the benefit of mankind.

Nor has Panama failed to benefit from the American presence in the Canal Zone. First and foremost, the United States has guaranteed the independence of Panama. The United States has provided a schedule of annual payments, successively raised from $250,000 to the present $1.9 million. Moreover, the Canal Company has been the chief employer of Panamanians and chief contributor to the Panamanian economy. We have always acted in the spirit of making fair adjustments, ever since the Hay-Bunau-Varilla Treaty of 1903.

This treaty was not a sudden development but the logical outgrowth of a series of historical events. The first of these was the report of January 18, 1902, by the Isthmian Canal Commission, headed by Rear Admiral John G. Walker, favoring the Panama Canal route rather than Nicaragua. This report recommended that "the grant of the Canal Zone must not be for a term of years, but in perpetuity, and a strip of territory from ocean to ocean of sufficient width must be placed under the control of the United States. In this strip the United States must have the right to enforce police regulations, preserve order, protect property rights, and exercise such other powers as are appropriate and necessary."

The next important move was the enactment of the Spooner Act, approved June 28, 1902, which, pursuant to the recommendations of the Walker Commission, authorized the President to acquire "perpetual control" of a canal strip from Colombia, to purchase the holdings of the French Panama Canal Co., and to construct the Panama Canal. In the event of inability to make a satisfactory treaty with Colombia, or to acquire the French holdings at a cost not exceeding $40 million, the act provided for construction of a canal in Nicaragua.

When the Colombian Senate refused to ratify the treaty, Panamanian leaders feared that, in spite of their hopes, they would lose the canal to Nicaragua. To avert that danger, on November 3, 1903, Panama seceded from Colombia and soon made a separate treaty with the United States, granting favorable terms as the inducement for selecting the Panama route. It was under this treaty that the Canal Zone was acquired, the Panama Canal constructed, and subsequently maintained, operated, sanitated, and protected.

Under the 1903 treaty, the United States undertook to guarantee and maintain the independence of Panama, paid Panama an indemnity of $10,000,-000 for the grants involved, assumed the obligation of the Panama Railroad for an annuity of $250,000, purchased all private land and property in the Canal Zone from individual owners, and established fortifications for the protection of the Canal. Panama granted in perpetuity the powers of sovereignty over the Canal Zone to the entire exclusion of the exercise of such powers by Panama, the right of eminent domain within the cities of Panama and Colon and the territory adjacent thereto, the right to enforce sanitary ordinances and maintain law and order in the terminal cities should Panama be unable to do so.

In 1936–1939 and 1955 treaties with Panama, the United States gave up the right of eminent domain in Panama, the authority to enforce sanitary ordinances and to maintain law and order in the terminal cities, and withdrew its activities to the boundaries of the Canal Zone.

We respected the natural desire of Panama to take over her own affairs as quickly as she became capable. Yet the one thing that would be to the detriment of both parties, would be for the United States to relinquish the sovereignty which we have necessarily exercised in the Canal Zone.

In January, 1964, communist-incited riots in Balboa and Panama City led to demands for complete revision of our relationship with Panama. President Johnson agreed to negotiate—and agreed that negotiations would begin with the assumption that the United States would surrender its perpetual sovereignty.

When the negotiations were completed in 1967, the treaties were a complete disaster. From the American point of view, there is only one way to describe their contents. These treaties proposed the greatest give-away since God gave man the world for his dominion. They wanted to give away United States jurisdiction and sovereignty. They contemplated giving away United States land, property, operating facilities, and engineering works. In short, they gave away the entire United States Canal—and indeed any new canal that the United States might build in Panama—to a dubious operating authority whose sole strength is the slender reed of promises by the Republic of Panama.

The first and most important of the proposed treaties was the basic renegotiated Panama Canal Treaty. It was to set up an organization described as an "international juridical entity" which would be the administrative agency for operating the Canal. All property there that then belonged to the United States Government would be turned over free of charge to the operating agency. The historic Canal Zone would be diminished from the ten-mile wide strip to an area approximately one mile wide. The Canal Administration would operate its own court system and its own police forces in the Canal area.

Obviously it is very crucial for the safety of the Canal to make sure that the United States has control. Ultimate control of the Canal under the proposed treaties would have been in a governing board of nine men. The United States would have a one-man majority on this board, but Congress would relinquish all control over the appointment of these men and would have no recourse if even one of them should turn out to be incompetent or to act against the best interests of the country.

Furthermore, the executive control would be in the hands of a Director General and his deputy. The terms of office of these men would alternate between the United States citizens and Panamanian citizens. At the present time, the President of the United States can assume direct control instantaneously if dangerous conditions warrant it. Under the five-four board, control would be so diluted that it would be impossible to be sure that effective action could be taken in time.

Another aspect of this treaty was that the formula for payments was strongly biased against the United States. Panama's share would be based on seventeen cents per long ton, going up to twenty-two cents year by year. After these payments are made, estimated to be about $20 million per year, then all other expenses of the Canal would be paid, including overhead, capital improvement, and operating funds. The last priority was held out for the United States payment, which is only eight cents per long ton and going up to ten cents. These increased payments could result in increased tolls which might easily be as high as twenty-five percent.

The second treaty was a status of forces treaty, which defined the rights and privileges of our military forces stationed to defend the Canal. One of the most serious drawbacks of this treaty was that it provided for a committee to confer when any special action is necessary to defend outbreaks of insurrection or enemy attack. It stipulated that in the event the committee fails to come to agreement on what measure can be taken, the controversy will be directed toward the respective governments through proper channels. It was an extremely cumbersome arrangement.

Another feature of this treaty was a provision that the Panamanian flag shall fly over all United States bases on Panamanian soil. The United States flag could not fly unless Panama gave special permission.

The third treaty proposes an option to build a so-called sea level canal somewhere in Panama. At that point no one knew whether a sea level canal would be technically or economically feasible. Congress had authorized a study which would take at least three years to complete.

When the treaty negotiators sat down two years ago, the United States held almost all the cards. We had, first of all, sovereignty—operating sovereignty in the Canal Zone. Secondly, we had won independence for Panama and furnished her with the main source of development and support. Thirdly, we have had a history of generous concessions and easy relations with Panama since the first treaty was signed in 1903.

The only card that Panama held was the somewhat dubious power of blackmail, a power growing out of extreme nationalist activities. There was absolutely no reason why a strong powerful nation like the United States should give in to the petty blackmail on the fluctuating Panamanian political scene. Yet when the negotiation game was over, Panama got up with the whole pot. We played as though we wanted to lose.

The spirited opposition which immediately rose up against these treaties gave the Administration second thoughts about bringing the treaties to the Senate for ratification. In Panama, extreme nationalism demanded the whole Canal, or nothing. In the tumultuous political situation, President Marco Robles did not dare sign the treaties he had accepted, since the Panamanian election campaigns were not far off. In the spring of 1968, Robles himself was impeached, only months before his term was over—raising questions of the stability and value of guarantees in treaties negotiated under such volatile circumstances. Significantly, legislation was introduced in both houses of Congress to modernize the existing facilities, expand their capacity, and modify their design according to the Third Locks-Terminal Lake Plan—a move which could be accomplished under the 1903 treaty.

This plan would increase the depth of the summit channel by five feet, regroup the locks at the Pacific end, and improve navigation by creating a terminal lake as a safe anchorage for vessels awaiting passage through the Pacific locks. Between 1939 and 1942, some $75 million was spent in planning and excavation for the unfinished Third Locks Plan, abandoned because of World War II. The current modernization proposals have important modifications, but would use most of this idle excavation to good advantage.

The modernized Panama Canal could handle all increases in traffic projected for this century. It could handle new and larger vessels. But best of all, the United States would own the improvements one-hundred percent, and have complete effective sovereignty over them. Our treaty relationship with Panama would remain exactly as before, with the Canal operation completely independent of Panama's own affairs. It is clear that a diminished American presence in the Canal Zone would be a provocative situation—an open invitation to attack and attempted take-over.

Nevertheless, in the eyes of the liberal press, we continued to be described as "colonialists." One of the greatest achievements of our history and technology was presented in the press as though it were a dirty little affair that had best be swept away.

Chapter VIII

THE DECLINE OF CONSTITUTIONAL GOVERNMENT

Civilization is not something that can be planned. It is an organic growth; the gradual accumulation of many labors and many individual attempts at perfection. Like any living organism, a civilization must struggle against enemies both without and within in order to remain free.

In practical terms, the three enemies of freedom are crime, collectivism, and communism. All three take away the liberty of the individual and destroy his security.

Crime is the attack of one individual upon another, and upon his rights. Collectivism is the attack of a power-hungry elite upon all individuals. Communism is the enemy of civilization itself, seeking to eradicate the very conditions of freedom.

Crime, collectivism, and communism are, each in turn, the three antagonists of life, liberty, and the pursuit of happiness.

Intent of Framers

The Declaration of Independence was a declaration of intent. The Founding Fathers wanted to set

142

up a nation where the dynamic balance of civilization could be established. The Constitution was the sensitive mechanism they eventually conceived to keep the enemies of freedom in check.

It is no coincidence that this nation's rising inability to deal with these threats coincides with the decline of constitutional government. The balance of powers set up in the Constitution is so delicate that it can be upset easily if the provisions of the Constitution are not rigidly adhered to.

The controlling factor in determining the meaning of the Constitution on any given issue is to study the historical evidence of the Framers' intentions. It is difficult to be too strict in construing the meaning of its terms.

Patrick Henry thought that the Constitution was unconstitutional; or at least he so argued before it was ratified.

"What right had they to say, *We, the People?*" he asked querulously. "Who authorized them to speak the language of *We, the People,* instead of *We, the States?* If the States be not agents of this compact, it must be one great consolidated national government of all the people of all the States. The people gave them no power to use their name. That they exceeded their authority is perfectly clear."

Once the Constitution was ratified, however, Patrick Henry defended it as the law of the land. But in the debates preceding ratification he feared that the Constitution left too much room for the development of a central tyranny of the same sort that the Americans had fought against in the Revolutionary War. He was suspicious, not of the motives of men who had drafted the Constitution in Philadelphia in good faith, but of the human inclination toward evil that can undermine the character of even the best public servant.

"The great and direct end of government is liberty," he warned. "Secure our liberty and privileges, and the end of government is answered. If this be not effectually done, government is an evil."

He who had spoken the first words of opposition to George III was just as quick to point out the dangers inherent in the provisions of the draft document. The Constitutional Convention had exceeded its authority, he said. He asserted that it had no power to change the form of the United States Government. Moreover, he felt that the form proposed did not contain enough safeguards against centralization of power.

Fellow patriots pointed out to him that the system proposed was a unique pattern of checks and balances. The States would retain their original authority; they were only delegating certain powers to the new government. The States would still be able to protect the individual from central tyranny. They pointed out that throughout the document the phrase, "the United States" is always *plural*.

"Treason against the United States, shall consist only in levying War against them, or in adhering to their Enemies, giving them Aid and Comfort." (Article III, Sect. 3.)

Against *them,* not *it.*

Finally, his friends mollified Patrick Henry by meeting his insistence upon a Bill of Rights. The last item in the Bill was the Tenth Amendment:

"The powers not delegated to the United States by the Constitution, nor prohibited by it to the

States, are reserved to the States respectively, or to the People."

Patrick Henry could not have known—but maybe he sensed—how this amendment would be interpreted. The Tenth Amendment is easily ignored by those who want to build up the central government. In 1936, the Supreme Court ruled that excise taxes on the sale of coal, produced by non-members of a coal code established as a part of a federal regulatory scheme, were found to invade the reserved powers of the States. Since then, the Supreme Court has not once called upon the Tenth Amendment to uphold state powers.

Concentration of Power

Some men fail to see danger in the concentration of power. They point to centralized government as more efficient. They say that a powerful government is able to do more for the people. They say that a strong central government is able to root out what they conceive to be local injustices. They say that our intricate and sophisticated society needs an extensive and comprehensive government to fulfill its needs.

Yet our Founding Fathers believed differently. They were afraid of efficiency without safeguards, because efficiency can make tyranny unbearable. They believed that people should primarily look to themselves to plan for and satisfy their wants. They knew that a strong central government is capable of perpetrating national injustices in the attempt to solve local minor problems. They knew that the danger of evil and corrupt leadership, hungry for power, was the greatest possible danger to personal freedom, no matter how intricate and sophisticated a society becomes. They planned both for the "separation of powers" in the Federal Government and the "division of powers" between the state governments and the Federal Government which the States held in common.

Separation of Powers

The "separation of powers," therefore, was not the product of mere whim or simplicity. The powers of government were separated in the Constitution for the purpose of preventing any single individual or group, including the people themselves, from gaining a monopoly on power. The object was to guarantee freedom by putting danger out of reach. The Founding Fathers had confidence that most men were fairly honest; but they also knew that there was no way of telling which men would betray that confidence.

Accordingly, the Constitution was an attempt to pit one faction against another, to play off strength against strength, and weakness against weakness. Every schoolboy is taught—or ought to be taught—about the familiar "separation of powers," and the three-part structure of the Federal Government. But we ought to be more aware that the principle of establishing opposing forces is found at every turn in the Constitutional structure.

For example: The Senate and the House of Representatives, respectively, were conceived to give fair representation to both size and sovereignty. At the same time, the biennial elections in the House pit the advantages of frequent elections against what was hoped to be the accumulated wisdom of the Senate.

The Senators were originally thought of as ambassadors, as it were, appointed by the legislature of the state sovereignties; it was, therefore, thought fitting that the Senate should give its "advise and consent" to national treaties. Members of the House were thought to be closer to the people because of their frequent election. Hence, the House was assigned the privilege of originating appropriation bills.

The point is that these functions were "separated" not for the sake of division, or to ease the burden, or merely to achieve a political compromise in the Constitutional Convention. The principle of separation was the need to balance power against power, initiative against initiative, function against funtion.

These examples show how, even within one branch of the government, the Founding Fathers envisioned a balance of powers. By multiplying that vision into the familiar triple plan of legislative, executive and judicial functions, each pitted against each other, the complex nature of the constitutional system becomes more evident.

At the same time, it is clear that each element of the Federal Government must see to it that it exercises its own functions effectively and decisively; but at the same time, each must seek to restrain itself within its own mandate. The duty of one branch is to check the other branch when it gets out of line; but self-restraint is always the most effective foundation of liberty.

Division of Powers

A description of the "separation of powers" in our Federal Government is not enough to explain our governmental system. The federal arrangements were spelled out by the Founding Fathers because something new was being created. Or rather, something new was being added on to a preexisting structure. The Federal Government was simply a small and relatively unimportant agency created for the ·common welfare of the States. The powers of government were not simply "separated" within the federal structure; they were also "divided" between federal functions and state functions.

The state governments, as the major seats of civil order, were expected to provide for the welfare of the people by instituting laws for their protection. The state governments were already rooted in the great tradition of English law. The state governments possessed the traditional "police powers" affecting the welfare of the individual citizen. The states possessed the court systems where persons went to right wrongs, and to secure justice. It was for this reason that a citizen exercised his right to vote within state jurisdiction, and conducted political affairs within state boundaries.

The Federal Government possessed no jurisdiction to legislate in matters of common law and common welfare. Its mandate, and its courts, extended only as far as the limited powers laid down by the Constitution. Under the Tenth Amendment to the Constitution, the Federal Government was empowered to legislate in only those fields of activity specifically delegated to it by the states. Those fields delegated to the Federal Government were the specific ones in which it was thought the Federal Government could render services to all the people better than any one state could do for its own people, or fields where a conflict of sovereignty might exist among the states.

In short, the states could legislate on any matter under the sun, except for a few specific matters handed over to the Federal Government, either in the original Constitution or in subsequent amendments. The Federal Government could legislate on no other.

Efficiency vs. Economy

No one could say that we have adhered to the plan laid down in the Constitution. Unfortunately, the arguments for so-called efficiency are winning out.

Only the Federal Government, it is said, has the tax resources and expertise to help the states with their problems. More and more, federal money buys the support of the big-city political machines, bypassing the state governments entirely.

Such aid, of course, must always be accompanied by guidelines. It is impossible to give money with no strings attached. The temptations of power are such that legitimate guidelines for true efficiency and proper accounting give way to policy guidelines, intended to limit the choices available to the recipients. As soon as the case for centralization is stated in this way, it is obvious that centralization, of necessity, restricts freedom.

Rivalry and competition, as the American system has proved, produce a kind of efficiency that goes beyond mere economy. They stimulate creativity and technological advances. With the increasing complexity of our civilization, this becomes even more important than it was in our agrarian past, to promote diversity. Despite the advances of computers and programming, no central authority can ever have adequate information to plan for every locality. Collectivism may at first appear to have the advantage in efficiency. But that kind of efficiency uses up the capital accumulated by past generations.

We must not only look at our government in terms of overall trends, but also in terms of specific changes. The Constitution has not only been ignored and distorted; in many cases it has been superseded. Entirely new structures have been erected in the shadow of the Constitution, and beyond. Many of the functions of government, particularly in policy-making, have been parceled out to executive agencies and to quasi-governmental corporations.

This shift, as important as the decline of the Constitution itself, marks a clear drive toward socialism and totalitarianism. It indicates that many of the most important functions of government are no longer subject to the people and their elected representatives. It is government by a technological elite.

In the United States, the nation is supposed to belong to the people. Congress represents the people in Washington. Congress is supposed to initiate the policies which the people want, subject to the limitations of the Constitution. The Executive role is to carry out the orders given by the people through their representatives.

But Congress has abdicated from its responsibility. In many respects, it has become an agency of the White House, routinely approving programs and appropriations sent down for confirmation.

Chapter IX

THE PROPER ROLE OF CONGRESS

Often the public image of the average member of Congress is not very flattering. Although some of the criticism leveled at the nation's lawmakers may be justified, it usually results from a misunderstanding of the congressman's tasks and the background in which he performs them.

The press can conjure an image which depicts the congressman as a good time Charlie, traveling around the world in Air Force jets, visiting glamorous foreign cities, and having big nights on the town with counterpart funds. Another view shows him as a pathetic, blundering, incompetent described so well in J. P. McEvoy's "My Congressman," which begins:

> I know I have a Congressman
>   in Washington, D.C.
> For now and then he comes around
>   to get a vote from me. . . .
> He proudly shakes me by the hand
>   And asks about my needs.
> And when he goes to Washington
>   He sends me garden seeds.

In reality, the average member of Congress is a hard-working, dedicated public servant. Perhaps his greatest dilemma is the selection of a basic method of operation. Should he simply reflect the will of the constituents who sent him to office? Or should he exercise independent judgment?

Generally speaking the more conservative-minded members of Congress tend toward the exercise of independent judgment. They act on the assumption (which is frequently verified by opinion polls) that the people are not fully aware of the issues. Consequently, conservatives believe that they were elected for the primary purpose of exercising their best judgment.

Regardless of the individual congressman's performance, the legislative body as a whole is subject to certain valid criticisms. An impartial assessment of Congress in the late 1960's reveals at least the following deficiencies:

Congress has—

1. Surrendered much of its power and prerogatives to the Executive Branch.
2. Failed to curb the power of the Supreme Court.
3. Legislated in areas never envisioned by the Constitution.
4. Failed to adopt necessary measures to clean its own house and to police its own activities.

Congress and the Executive Branch

In the history of our country the power relationship between the President and the Congress has had many ups and downs, reflecting generally the strength of the personalities involved. If this relationship were plotted as a curve, it would show peaks and valleys about a fairly level average of activity from the Administrations of George Washington through that of Herbert Hoover. With the inauguration of Franklin D. Roosevelt we began having more of a "presidential" government than a "congressional" one. After 1933 the peaks and valleys of the power relationship would continue, but the overall slant of the curve would be up toward the President's side.

Since then, the Executive Branch has increased tremendously in size and importance. Some expansion was pure and simple "empire building," some was really needed to meet changing times and conditions.

At the end of World War II there were sixty "departments" in our government. Not all were under the President—the Library of Congress and the Government Printing Office, for example. Since that time more have been created, together with a number of other new agencies. These jointly form the "Fourth Dimension" of government discussed in Chapter III.

The significant expansion of the Executive Branch has been paralleled by another phenomenon that was not envisioned by the Founding Fathers, but which has given the Executive a great deal more power—the Defense Establishment.

For the past two decades, the United States has had to maintain large, standing armed forces. This is one of the most radical changes in America, and it has been accepted at its face value as a twentieth-century fact of life. The maintenance of these forces —necessary as they may be—creates economica and political problems not foreseen in the Constitu tion. It also gives the party in office unprecedented advantages.

Defense has become a definite part of our society. It is big; it is everywhere; it is expensive—and it is commanded by the President, the Commander-in-Chief.

The influence of Defense reaches into almost every part of the country. Each neighborhood has something military: an arsenal, a depot, shipyard, hospital, air field, training center, fort or recruiting station. Defense contracts and military pay rolls are important economic factors in many communities.

The Commander-in-Chief of this vast military system wields great power:

1. He develops and controls the Defense budget —over fifty percent of the national budget.

2. He can order troops to enforce laws (as at Little Rock or Oxford) or he can use troops to suppress civil disorder (as at Detroit or the Pentagon).

3. He can involve the country in hostilities without consulting Congress. (As in Korea or Vietnam.)

4. He can use classified military facts and manage military news to his advantage.

An example of presidentially managed news occurred early in 1968. As reported in the *New York Times* of January 1, 1968, the Administration had exerted considerable pressure in late 1967 to obtain optimistic reports of progress in South Vietnam. The story began:

> American officials at almost all levels, both in Saigon and in the provinces, say they are under steadily-increasing pressure from Washington to produce convincing evidence of progress, especially by the South Vietnamese,

in the next few months. The pressure began
to increase about three months ago, the officials report, and became more intense in
December. They expect no lessening, and probably a further increase as the American elections approach.

In speaking of the so-called "Washington squeeze
play," one official said that he was told, "An election year is about to begin. And the people we work
for are in the business of re-electing President Johnson in November."

Some of the officials reported that they were
afraid to tell Washington the truth for fear of losing
their jobs.

Perhaps it was this squeeze play that led President Johnson to say in his State of the Union message that, "The number of South Vietnamese living
in areas under government protection tonight has
grown by more than a million since January of last
year." But what kind of "protection"?

Shortly afterward, thousands of dead civilians,
casualties of the 1968 TET offensive in South Vietnam, were mute evidence of the fallacy of that protection.

Because of the significant civilian and military
extension of his office, the President now is the
leading participant in the legislative function. He has
the largest staff in the government to prepare the
annual President's Budget and Legislative Program.
The Executive Branch not only proposes most of the
legislation upon which Congress is to act, but also
furnishes the language of the bills. The main law-
making business of the Congress is presently re-

duced to discussing, modifying or (sometimes) rejecting White House proposals.

Despite the great increase in presidential power, the Congress still has some restraining measures. It retains money power over all of the programs submitted to it. The Congress still retains its investigating authority, and the Senate has power of confirmation. At present these are the best defenses that Congress has against Executive encroachment of its prerogatives, and they are the primary means by which the Legislative Branch could mount an offensive to recapture some of its lost authority, prestige, and independence.

Congress and the Supreme Court

From time to time there have been conflicts between the Congress and the Supreme Court. As early as 1803 the Supreme Court established its authority to declare an act of Congress unconstitutional; since that first occasion the Court has reasserted this right at least eighty times. Congress never seriously challenged the Court in any of these issues, but it has, in a number of instances, enacted statutes intended to modify the effect of such rulings by the court. The Court, in turn, has also found some of these modifying statutes to be unconstitutional.

Many authorities assert that the Court has moved into areas of decision that were originally envisioned by the Constitution as the Congress' prerogative. Whether or not the Court made these moves to fill a void, some of its more recent decisions impinge on legislative areas that should be a primary responsibility of Congress.

One example of this "usurpation" is the Supreme

Court's decision against prayer in the schools. The Constitution was never meant to forbid public prayer or to deny God a place in the ritual of the school day—the Judicial Branch notwithstanding. As a result of the rulings on prayer, which many Americans regard as judicial nonsense, some legislators introduced a constitutional amendment to clear up the situation and reaffirm the American right to choose prayer in the schools. This amendment is now pending in the Constitution Amendment Subcommittee of the Senate Judiciary Committee.

In the Court's one-man-one-vote apportionment decisions, the Congress failed in its duty to protect the intent of the Constitution. In this instance, the Court's decision is so manifestly wrong that thirty-two states have now called for a Constitutional Convention to rewrite the Constitution as it was intended. When just two more states present resolutions, such a Constitutional Convention will be possible—the first time since the Constitution was written in Philadelphia in 1787.

As the Supreme Court renders decision after decision that remakes America through its interpretation of the "living" Constitution, the public has shown more and more uneasiness. There is a growing feeling among the people, and many of the Legislative Branch, that the Supreme Court has gone too far and must be checked. This is best expressed by these words of Thomas Jefferson: "There is no danger I apprehend so much as the consolidation of our government by the noiseless, and therefore, unalarming, instrumentality of the Supreme Court."

In its contest with the Supreme Court, Congress is fighting a losing battle at present. The only power Congress has chosen to exert over the Court is the power of confirmation. Nevertheless, other means of curbing the Court could be enacted with little modification or damage to age-old customs and tradition.

Aside from the power of impeachment, Congress has the power to propose a constitutional amendment to the states to limit the term of office of the members of the Supreme Court, or to provide that Supreme Court Justices be reconfirmed periodically as Congress determines. These remedies would obviate the politically difficult impeachment procedure, which is the only avenue currently available for the removal of a justice. It is seldom used; within the over all court system in the United States, only four judges have been impeached—and none from the Supreme Court.

The Constitution provides Congress with another remedy to check the Supreme Court. Congress has not seen fit to use it, but Article III, Section II provides the authority, to wit: "In all the other Cases before mentioned, the Supreme Court shall have appellate jurisdiction, both as to Law and Fact, with such exceptions, and under such Regulations as the Congress shall make." In other words, Congress could pass a statute removing the fields desired from the jurisdiction of the Supreme Court.

Another example would be the enactment of a statute to establish an age limit for the Justices, requiring their retirements at age 70 or 75. The effect of such an age limitation on the present Supreme Court can be seen from the ages of the Justices in 1968: Warren, 76; Black, 81; Douglas, 68; Harlan, 68; Brennan, 61; Marshall, 59; Fortas, 57; White, 50; Stewart, 52.

In some cases, Congress can overcome the effect of particular decisions by statutory enactment. For example, when the Court holds federal action has preempted a certain field, Congress can subsequently pass legislation declaring it has not preempted the authority of the states to legislate in such field. Of course, some Supreme Court decisions—such as the school prayer and legislative apportionment cases—may require constitutional amendments.

It has been suggested that Congress submit a constitutional amendment to the states setting additional qualifications for Supreme Court Justices. For example, only persons with five years service on the highest trial court in a state or on a court with appellate jurisdiction would be eligible for appointment. This would limit membership on the Supreme Court to experienced judges, and prevent purely political appointments.

From the earlier discussion of recent trends in Supreme Court decisions in Chapter II, it is clear that Congressional action will be necessary if the Supreme Court's influence is to be curbed. As mentioned, several courses of action are available to the Congress. The failure of Congress to act in this important area has only encouraged the Supreme Court to continue its policy of handing down decisions disruptive to the order and security of our society.

Legislation that Exceeds the Bounds of the Constitution

In the opinion of many members of Congress, as well as officials in state governments, the Congress exceeded the bounds of the Constitution when it began to legislate in the fields of education and civil rights.

Generally speaking, Congress operates without any form of executive or judicial reviews of its actions. Normally a judicial review occurs when someone contests the legality of enacted legislation through the nation's courts. Otherwise, it is assumed that individual legislators perform a quasi-review by asking themselves the following question when considering legislation: "What provision of the Constitution of the United States authorizes the Congress to enact this bill into law?"

It is just as much the responsibility and duty of the Legislative Branch to consider and determine the constitutionality of bills proposed for enactment, as it is that of the Supreme Court to determine the constitutionality of statutes.

Since 1957, the succession of civil rights proposals that tended to expand the power of the Federal Government provide the best examples of legislation that exceed the bounds of the Constitution. With these proposals, the Congress has undertaken to replace and supersede state legislatures in entering the domain rights that are concerned with life, liberty, and property.

The Civil Rights Act of 1964 contained far-reaching and unconstitutional sections dealing with public accommodations, federal fund withholding, and FEPC. The Voting Rights Act of 1965 arrogated certain criteria for voting, and specifically authorized illiterates to vote, in violation of state laws and constitutions which have jurisdiction of these matters under the United States Constitution.

It remained for the President's Civil Rights Package of 1967-1968 to show how some political factions prefer so-called "civil rights" more than justice itself. In their zeal, the proponents of this package ignored some of the basic guarantees of the Constitution.

With this package, the civil rights advocates were trying to bend and distort the Fourteenth Amendment. They hoped to extend the power of the Federal Government into the control of private activities. Under the theory of this legislation, there is no rational stopping point for the surge of federal power over the individual lives and conduct of private citizens.

Congress Must Clean Its Own House

Twenty-two years ago, the 79th Congress enacted the Legislative Reorganization Act of 1946. This provided the Legislative Branch with an organization that at best was less cumbersome than before. Its principal work was to reduce the number of standing committees from eighty-one to thirty-four, and to give the committees permanent professional staffs and clerical assistants.

Despite the reorganization and the well-meaning efforts of these permanent staffs, Congress still is slow to respond to public opinion and to react to new problems. Negativism runs deep. Congress needs better ways to deal with the Executive Branch and to manage its own work load more efficiently.

The functions of Congress are mainly to (1) make the laws (legislate) and (2) to control the purse strings (appropriate). Under present procedures, both of these functions are carried out simultaneously. As a consequence, the authorization bill for a program may not be passed until after the appropriation is enacted. The difference in timing necessitates a supplemental or additional appropriation bill.

This illustrates one of the factors contributing to confusion on the Hill. Congress meets on a calendar year basis; government bookkeeping is done on a fiscal year basis—from July 1 to June 30th. As a result, many of the major appropriation bills are not enacted by Congress until well after the beginning of the fiscal year for which the appropriation is to be used. To cover the gap, Congress usually adopts a "continuing resolution," which permits spending by the agency affected at the level authorized for the previous fiscal year. In the press of time to get legislation enacted under this cumbersome system, many items which otherwise would get careful study and thought, receive only cursory attention.

The depth and complexity of the national budget is beyond the scope of the Congress. Few Congressmen or committee staffs can examine it in critical detail. Moreover, the format of the budget, as well as format changes, makes it very difficult to trace items from year to year. If it wished, Congress could prescribe a "standard" budget format and make other federal agencies use it.

As a means of better examination and interpretation of budget matters, the Congress could adapt the budget to computerization. Further, it could employ systems analysts for deeper evaluation.

In its relations with the Executive Branch, Congress should examine the exercise of emergency powers by the President. This practice, which has grown steadily over the past hundred years, is used to justify actions which would normally require legislation. Another important area that needs examination and corrective action is the extent to which the Executive Branch flouts the will of the Congress. This is not an open rebellion—it is accomplished with smoothness and polish in any one of several ways.

For Congress to reassert its authority and independence, it must desist from compliance with the wishes of the Executive. It must develop less sensitivity to the condemnation or approval by the news media, which delights in keeping a "box score" of the status of the President's legislative program.

There is still a lot of work to do to straighten out the committee system. Committee work is important. It is the best means whereby a few members of the Congress can investigate a subject in depth and make a knowledgeable report to their colleagues. But the problems of jurisdiction and committee chairman need to be resolved. The committee system would work better if there were a mandatory retirement age for chairmen, and if the chairmanship were rotated among several of the top majority members.

Committee jurisdiction is a knotty problem. Take the matter of Defense procurement as an example. The Committees on Government Operations of both Houses have jurisdiction over the Federal Property and Administrative Services Act. The respective Armed Services Committees have jurisdiction over the Armed Services Procurement Act; but jurisdiction over the Renegotiation Act, which bears on Defense and other procurement, is under the jurisdiction of the Ways and Means Committee of the House of Representatives and the Finance Committee in the Senate.

Furthermore, the Walsh-Healy Public Contracts Act and the Service Contract Act of 1965, also involving procurement and contracting processes, are under the jurisdiction of the Education and Labor Committee of the House, and the Labor and Public Welfare Committee of the Senate. The Banking and Currency Committee handles small business legislation, but there is also a Small Business Committee that investigates procurement problems from the small business—not the government's—side of the street. Patent and claims legislation, which also influence procurement and contracting matters, are within the jurisdiction of the Judiciary Committee. At the same time there are separate and different committees responsible for atomic energy legislation on the one hand, and for space legislation on the other.

Federal procurement for goods, services, equipment, and facilities now runs about $60 billion a year. How can procurement be handled efficiently when there is such confusion over jurisdiction, and when so many committees are in the act?

Then there is the question of campaign reform. This involves:

1. The problem of pricing out of the political marketplace those candidates who are unable to finance their own campaigns.
2. The problem of making less-affluent candidates wholly dependent on financial support by vested interests.

Probably the best solution would be for Congress to enact legislation to encourage contributions from as broad a spectrum of the citizens as possible—on a purely voluntary basis. Each individual should have the opportunity to support the candidate of his choice. The encouragement for a contribution might be established in the form of a deduction from taxable income for a *limited* contribution to the campaign of a bona fide candidate for a political office. Each candidate receiving contributions could set up a committee to disburse the funds in his behalf.

In 1967 the Senate passed and sent to the House a new Legislative Reorganization Act designed to update Congressional rules and procedures. It included many reforms but overlooked others. One of the most basic considerations is almost always overlooked: *Congress should voluntarily cut back in the areas in which it chooses to legislate.*

The basic theory of our Constitution is that Congress legislates only on those matters delegated to it by the states. As long as Congress tries to legislate on all of the ills of mankind, leaving almost nothing for consideration by the states, the work load in Congress will be exorbitant, and the caliber of work accomplished will be inferior. If there were fewer items on the agenda, a reorganized, independent Congress could reassert its dominant role as the representative of the people.

Should the members of Congress fail to enact meaningful reforms, continue to muddle along with business as usual, and continue to play second fiddle to the Executive and Judiciary Branches, they will deserve the bumbling image that is now held by some of the people.

Chapter X

WHAT GOVERNMENT MUST DO

America was still a small land when Francis Scott Key posed the question we have never forgotten: Does the Star Spangled Banner yet wave over the land of the free and the home of the brave?

Key had no doubts; he was asking a rhetorical question. For the proud and confident Americans of his era, it was unthinkable that the flag should not wave.

In our own day, when we are the mightiest nation on earth, and the most prosperous, the question is posed in different terms. The Star Spangled Banner is the symbol of our nation, and it waves in recognition of our dominion. The question today is whether our power will continue, or fall into decline. More importantly, the question is whether, if the banner continues to wave, it will wave over the land of the free.

The nation that ceases to expand its consciousness begins to die at that very moment. Once a nation loses its conviction of truth, doubts and self-doubts rob it of its will and its strength. Such a nation declines as a moral influence in the world, and as a force with which to be reckoned.

167

Britain

America has before it the example of Britain, no longer to be called great.

Since Rome ruled the world, no nation has had the genius and strength to equal her feat, except Britain.

Since Rome governed the barbarians, no nation has imposed civilization and law upon global anarchy in the same manner as Britain. Little Britain became Great Britain because it was great in its intangible spirit. Toward the middle of Queen Victoria's reign, Britain awoke to find it had an empire, even though it had never intended to assemble one.

But it was not long before the British Empire nurtured within itself the seeds of its own destruction. The prosperity of the empire proved a temptation to those who thought that man's life was bound up in the pursuit of material goods. The failure of spiritual understanding led to crass acquisitiveness by some—and, worse yet, a conviction on the part of others that social ills and poverty could be alleviated by state action to confiscate the capital accumulated by private citizens. Socialism—the welfare state—was born.

The failure of Britain's welfare state today is not merely an economic failure. It is a failure of spirit. Britain can no longer afford to support her empire or her world responsibilities; ironically, she can no longer afford the welfare luxuries she chose when she consciously gave up her global role. The welfare state encouraged many of her most talented and energetic people to leave. Britain's industries are plagued by low productivity and poor quality. Today Britain is a land of embittered intellectuals and frank featherbedders. The nation that was once the very epitome of courage, justice, liberty and experience, now projects the image of the narcissistic teen-age reveler.

These words are written more in compassion than in condemnation, for Britain now appears to have no road back. It is evident that the United States suffers from many of the same ills. In the book *Cold Friday,* published posthumously a few years ago, Whittaker Chambers made this observation: "The West is swayed by a profound will to die. . . . Actually, and with the profoundest vindictiveness of unhealth, it does not wish to be defended; it deeply resents anyone who would defend it and will seek to destroy him . . . because it cannot be defended without facing the truth about itself. Nor can anyone truly defend it without, ultimately, speaking the truth about it. That it cannot stand and so, first of all, it must long to destroy those who would save it."

Only time will tell whether Chambers' conclusion is accurate, but it is doubtful that the events of the years since he recorded his observation would have shaken his belief. It may well be that our society will not now face the truth, or permit the truth about itself to be presented. Yet Chambers also admitted, in his words, that "truth has become the one consuming need, since nothing else has real worth."

The Road Back

If America is to retain its power to do good in the world, our government must immediately reform itself. Government can do little to reform its citizens, but it does have the power of reforming itself. Our government must reform both its policies and its laws.

Our policies—the goals of government—must be realigned on three fronts. Foremost must be a return to the constitutional framework envisioned by our forefathers. The technology of transportation and communications has made the dangers of centralization and usurpation of power even more critical than when we were an agricultural nation. Times change, but human nature does not. The insight of the Framers into human nature was so precise that their principles transcend the complexities of social and scientific change. The structure of local government and local problems today is infinitely varied, exceeding the scope of Washington bureaucrats' solutions. The Federal Government will be strengthened, if it divests itself of activities which are beyond its legal writ and practical ability.

In order to achieve constitutional government, the courts must once more adopt the principle that the *historical intent* of the framers of legislation, or of the Constitution, must be the controlling factor in interpretation. If law is not constant, there is no law.

Strengthen the States

The second point is that the state governments must be strengthened so as to encourage diversified policies independent of federal control. The states must not be allowed to become administrative units of the Federal Government. They should be the initiators of new policies and new concepts. It is not true to say that the state governments do not have the resources that are available to the Federal Government. The problem is that the Federal Government has preempted the field of taxation in such a way as to make it difficult for the states to apply levies that are suitable to their needs.

State taxation at the present time is only at levels that are a fraction of the federal tax rates. No state dares to raise its rates significantly above those of other states, for such action would cause an outflow of individuals and businesses, thus retarding the state's economic growth. Some mechanism is necessary to enable the states to raise their tax income without imposing extra burdens upon their own people. The simplest way to do this is an amendment to the federal taxation system which would return tax revenues to the states without strings attached. Thus the states would be able to increase their level of services and develop their own programs, enabling the Federal Government to withdraw from many of the fields it has invaded.

It stands to reason that the Federal Treasury gets its money from the same taxpayers as the state treasuries.

Those who argue that the Federal Government has greater resources than the states, overlook an important fact: People frequently have to pay additional state and local taxes, in order to qualify for federal subsidies for which they have already been taxed at the federal level. The reason is that two-thirds of all federal subsidies are available only on a matching grant basis. The estimated amount of federal subsidies to the states in 1967 was $8.047 billion. In order to receive these monies, the state and local governments had to levy increased local taxes to qualify for the matching grants.

Those who say that the federal government can more easily increase taxes than state and local governments are actually citing the most telling arguments against their position. The truth is that the state governments are closer to the people and are more sensitive to the popular demand for economy, while the Federal Government with its gigantic bureaus and political log-rolling is more distant from the retribution of the taxpayers.

Returning tax money to the states in the form of bloc grants would not make it more difficult to raise taxes, but would at least see to it that tax money was spent more efficiently for the true needs of the citizens.

Free the Citizen

Finally, the citizen at the local level must be freed from the effects of government benevolence, so that he may be politically and economically independent. The citizen who is incapable of supporting himself and his dependents cries out for humanitarian assistance. There will always be those who are mentally or physically disabled, and who are bona fide charity or welfare cases. The public can and should take care of them. Even those who are able to work, but unable to find employment, cannot be left to starve in misery. The social conditions which grow out of such misery are an unwanted burden upon the rest of the citizens. But work is preferable to welfare.

The effects of receiving government welfare payments eventually undermine the character of even the most determined and hard-working personality. If the best of men are harmed by crippling support, how much more so are those harmed who have inadequate educational preparation or weak character formation? Thus we witness a spectacle of soaring costs of public welfare and increasing numbers of welfare clients. In 1950, national welfare costs amounted to $2.4 billion and the number of Americans getting public assistance was six million. In 1967, the same figures had risen in a steep curve to $7.6 billion in aid with 8.4 million recipients.

Some so-called experts are saying today that work is an old-fashioned idea; they say that the age of computers and automatic machinery will so drastically reduce the number of workers needed that the government will have to support the majority of people without requiring them to work. These experts say that we will have to revise our attitudes about the dignity of labor, and our disapproval of those who do not work. The theory even goes so far as to say that it will be the duty of the government to provide entertainment and constructive hobbies for those who are permanently idle.

In the time since these theories were first voiced a number of years ago, events have not borne out the predictions. Automation seems to increase the total job market, instead of throwing everyone out of work—although of course many other factors enter into job availability in a given locality. The picture of life without work, painted by the supposed experts, seems to have vanished.

Despite this setback, however, there is a growing tendency to accept the no-work philosophy. Welfare consultants are now propounding the idea that welfare payments are a "right," which is to be placed alongside the rights to life, liberty, and the pursuit of happiness. Washington, D. C., was recently the scene of the first Convention of the National Organization for Welfare Rights, consisting of delegates who were living on welfare and were meeting together to discover ways to increase so-called welfare rights. One delegate boasted to the press that she had reared five children on welfare, and that her children were rearing her grandchildren on welfare. Nevertheless, she seemed to feel that she was being cheated of still more benefits which she deserved.

When welfare benefits are considered "rights," instead of charity, then human dignity is compromised. A person demanding such amazing "rights" becomes arrogant and irresponsible. If such a person is able to work, but won't, he becomes confirmed in his idleness. In caring for the general welfare, government, at some level, should see to it that some form of work is available to those who cannot get employment in our free enterprise system. Any such work provided by the government should restrict wages to a figure less than that generally available in the open market, in order to provide an incentive for the employee to leave the government payroll. Those who are able to work should earn their own living. This course would alleviate the necessity for unemployment compensation which pays people to do nothing. When the government pays people to do nothing, it destroys incentive and inspires idleness.

Nevertheless, government should never take over the major responsibility for providing work. As long as those who can't work, or are unable to find work, are on the fringe of society, the nation will be productive enough to provide some surplus to help them. On the other hand, once the attitude of no-work pervades all classes of society, then the nation will become sterile and non-productive.

Unfortunately, the no-work philosophy is not confined to those receiving public assistance. The largesse of the Federal Government corrupts all those upon whom it showers unearned benefits. Many government programs are established in order to help those who are in real need, but others have become a boondoggle, enriching those who could not get rich in any other way. Every senator and every congressman is familiar with the hundreds of requests he receives daily for assistance in receiving this or that benefit from the Federal Treasury. The senators and congressmen are eager to help those with legitimate requests, but it is discouraging to see the number of citizens who expect the government to give them something for nothing.

Thus, at each of the three levels of government—federal, state and community—and finally, at the level of the individual citizen himself, our national policy must be to return each to an attitude of self-restraint and active responsibility.

Fortify Independence

Just as our domestic goals must be realigned in order to re-establish our independence, so too, our goals in foreign policy must be rewritten to fortify our independence and sovereignty. Our first goal must be to implant a dominant influence in world affairs. We must cease to apologize for our success and for our economic and military might. We must re-establish the conviction of our own integrity and demonstrate that we are ready to accept the responsibilities of our power. Other nations have learned to despise us because we refrain from using our strength in a just and humane manner. A nation which has no sense of honor has no influence in the world.

Our second goal in foreign policy is a corollary of the first. We must seek to help the underdeveloped nations develop their potential by teaching them the principles which made America strong and great. We must show them that they must avoid directed political and economic systems, so-called guided democracy and planned economy. We must encourage them to see how political power must be divided, if it is to be dynamic and if it is to create the spark of life which distinguishes progressive society. We must show them that the best way to get the most out of their limited capital is to set up structures to encourage individual incentive and initiative. Finally, we must teach them to spread development throughout their country and not from a small capital alone, and that responsibilities and political power must be distributed by means of regional arrangements.

The third goal is that we must seek to bring about the collapse of communism wherever it has gained a foothold in the world. We must never forget that the communists are our enemies and that in every communist country, the people are captives of the communist elite. There will be no peace and security in the world until the leadership in the captive nations, including those nations which make up the gigantic Soviet empire, is no longer communist.

Nazi Germany was once our bitter enemy, an enemy of all decent civilization. Yet, after the downfall of the leadership of the country, Germany became a friend and a warm ally of which we have never ceased to be proud.

So too, it is foolish to expect leaders molded by ideologies and blind hatred to mellow or change their point of view, when we give them no reason to force them to do it. There is every reason to believe that the Soviet peoples, the Chinese, the Eastern European nations, the Cubans, and others trapped under socialist tyranny, will once more be our friends, particularly if we assist them in getting rid of the tyrannical regimes that hold them captive.

Nevertheless, it is not government alone that can return us to the road back.

Chapter XI

WHAT THE CITIZEN CAN DO

In these times of great confusion and controversy, more and more Americans are asking, "What can we do?"

Puzzled, angered and frustrated, they wonder what they can do about the great troubles of the day. Can their views, opinions and support mean anything in the fight against inflation, crime, riots, communism and the slow disintegration of our constitutional form of government?

The answer is an unqualified "Yes." The individual citizen can do something to save this country.

In our democratic form of government nothing is more important than the views and beliefs of the individual. The views of the majority will prevail. In this regard, however, it has been wisely said that, "The beginning of wisdom in democratic theory is to distinguish between the things the people can do and the things the people cannot do."

A great deal of this book already has been devoted to the things that the people should not do:

1. They should not take the law in their own hands.
2. They should not vote for increasingly greater welfare programs.

3. They should not permit the Federal Government to destroy or replace local institutions by central planning.

Now it is time to consider a few of the things that the people can, and *should* do.

Lessons of the Past

First, we might do a little reflective thinking about what we want out of life, the principles we hold dear, and the sacrifices we may have to make to attain our goals. In this regard, we might look briefly at the past, and compare conditions in our country with the experience of others to see if there are any lessons to be learned.

Historians tell us that the downfall of a great civilization is usually preceded by the disappearance of civic spirit and initiative, and the devaluation of those things that once bound the people together. Some think that this is what is now happening to America. They believe that the United States has reached its zenith, and is now undergoing a process of slow decay. The American people, they say, particularly those in crowded cities and sprawling suburbs, are finding it difficult to identify with the community. Consequently, Americans are following the same patterns of behavior that marked the decline of other great power civilizations.

Studies of history show that the average age of the world's great governments has been 200 years, and that the general steps through which they progressed and regressed were: From bondage to spiritual faith; from spiritual faith to great courage; from courage to liberty; from liberty to abundance;

from abundance to complacency; from complacency to apathy; from apathy to dependency; and from dependency back again to bondage.

The five basic reasons given by Gibbon in his *Decline and Fall of the Roman Empire* for the death of that great civilization are also worthy of note. As Gibbon listed them, the reasons were: 1. the undermining of the dignity and sanctity of the home— the basis of all human society; 2. higher and higher taxes to fund the spending of public money for free bread and circuses for the people; 3. the mad craze for pleasure; 4. the building of great armaments for the defeat of an external enemy when the real enemy was within; 5. the decay of individual morality and responsibility; and 6. the decay of religion, faith fading into mere form, losing touch with life and its power to guide the people.

It must be left to individual judgment whether and where our nation falls into the ladder of life of the average great government, and whether there is a parallel between the reasons isolated by Gibbon as responsible for the decline and fall of the Roman Empire and the state of our own society.

The Modern Challenge

Unfortunately, the forces of atheistic materialism are not conveniently confined within the communist bloc or even excluded from our shores. What other reason than the dedication to atheistic materialism here in our own society can account for our failure to inspire the nations of the world with the spiritual values of liberty and free enterprise, instead of our accepted traditional policy of attempting to light a guiding beacon powered by inert materialism? Do we fear to offer the world more than greater material abundance, because in so doing we might have to admit to ourselves that the foundation of our own society has been shifted from spiritual values to materialistic clay? Do we refrain from pointing out to the peoples of the world the fallacies and tragic results of atheistic materialism underlying socialist philosophy, because we fear too much of the criticism might be applicable to our own society?

It has been well said that the greatness or weakness of any society depends, in the final analysis, on the outlook and attitude of the individuals who comprise it. It follows that the course and destiny of a society depend on the individual.

This is particularly true in the United States today. No longer is there a strong and balanced two party system in the Congress to moderate the excesses of a political majority. If there is to be a moderation of our course, much less a return to original values envisioned by the Constitution, the direction must come from the people themselves. Under existing circumstances, this will require something little less than a miraculous change in the sense of responsibility and capacity for effective expression previously evidenced by our society.

In the final analysis, it is not only the fate of our society which is at stake, but a final judgment on each of our personal lives. In considering this judgment, it is not amiss that we consider the judgment of the Church in Laodicea, which was in these words from the Book of Revelations: "I know thy works; thou art neither cold nor hot; I would thou wert cold or hot. So then because thou art lukewarm, and neither cold nor hot, I will spew thee out of my mouth. Because thou sayest, I am rich, and increased with goods, and have need of nothing; and knowest not that thou art wretched, and miserable, and poor, and blind, and naked."

Can we, or will we, escape the same judgment?

The way for those of us who choose to avoid such a judgment is clear, but demanding.

We must choose to fight for a recognition of the supremacy of God in national and individual affairs, for without Divine guidance we can accomplish nothing.

We must choose to fight for a return to the Constitution, for it is the best political charter yet devised by which men can govern themselves.

We must choose to fight for freedom, for without it our existence is meaningless.

We must choose to fight for honesty and integrity, in private and in public life, for without them our society is doomed to degradation.

We must choose to fight for law and order, for in the absence of law and order, society is reduced to mob rule.

We must choose to fight to keep the United States strong militarily, for without superior military power we cannot maintain both freedom and peace; but in so doing, we must keep ever in mind that within ourselves are potentially our most dangerous enemies—spiritual poverty, preoccupation with materialism, complacency, and apathy.

The Old-Fashioned Virtues

Many believe we are in deep trouble, but the prophets of American doom are badly mistaken.

If there is one lesson to be learned from forty years of public life, it is this: Never underestimate the American public. In a lifetime of public service, one talks to or corresponds with hundreds of thousands of individual citizens across the country. The average American is not as far removed from his pioneer ancestors as most people think. Though he lives in different surroundings, and has a veneer of twentieth-century sophistication, he is basically a hard-working, God-fearing person who believes in himself and his country. Perhaps he does not go around discussing his beliefs, but he has a great appreciation for the worthwhile values of society, and the old-fashioned virtues of independence, initiative, industry, respect for law and order, and faith in God.

We must not despair over the so-called moral deterioration in America. Each generation in this country has had its recalcitrants whose antics and protests received unwarranted publicity. In the long run the shallow views and the questionable behavior of this minority disappeared, leaving only a trace of influence on the character and lives of their contemporaries. The current "hippie" craze is probably already on its way out, only to be replaced by some other new adolescent philosophy just as disturbing. As with the other similar philosophies of protest, these will wash against the sturdy pillars of decent society, create some turbulence, and recede in the resulting undertow. The values of old-fashioned virtues are too fully ingrained in the American populace to suffer much damage from such lightweight fads and fancies.

Hope for the Future

But the United States is moving headlong down the path to the superstate. The growth of big government, the encroachment on individual liberties, and the usurpation of power by the Federal Government are documented beyond question. The easiest path for the individual citizen is to relax, and let the forces at work continue without interference or protest.

But this is not the answer. The preservation of our liberties and the retention of our free enterprise will depend upon an alert populace. The people will have to guard their rights jealously, and must stop hoping that some great leader will arise to lead us out of difficulty. We should not expect a presidential Moses. No one man is going to save us.

If we are going to be saved, if we are going to protect our individual freedom, and if we are going to retain our system of free enterprise, it will be the "average American" who does it. The poor are unable and the rich unwilling.

By exercising his power at the ballot box, by taking an active community interest and by speaking out for his beliefs, this average American can return sanity to our government. He can express the discontent of law-abiding citizens who are getting sick and tired of bureaucrats catering to lawless minorities. He can insist on less federal spending and a reduction of the size of the Washington bureaucracy. He can demand a cutback in the great give-away programs, and more emphasis on dignified work. He can become his brother's neighbor—not his keeper.

We must look to the American voter, the responsible citizen, to halt the trend toward superstatism. By a jealous watch over the domain of each level of government—local, state, and federal—he can halt the trend to destroy state sovereignty and to make the fifty states administrative units of the Federal Government.

We must discard the false hope that the greatest external threat to our security—international communism—is "mellowing," and remain ever watchful against this Godless movement until it abandons its dreams of world domination.

Above everything, we must realize that all Americans, no matter what race, color or creed, have an investment in the future of America. Each is entitled to earn and enjoy his own part of the American heritage. Because of this purpose the United States was founded. Because of this dream America has prospered.

The bedrock for all our expectations, the Constitution of the United States of America, exacts stern compliance with its provisions and demands faith in its policies. When we fail to observe this discipline, we stray from the course our forefathers charted for greatness. When we exchange freedom for personal security we deny the blessings of liberty to ourselves and our posterity.

We must return to the vision of the Founding Fathers or our children will suffer because of the faith we have not kept.

INDEX

HELP GET THIS BOOK TO OTHERS!

IT WILL HELP THEM DECIDE WHAT THEY CAN DO!

This book should be in every
American home.

Every American who loves liberty
and the opportunity a free America
has provided should give this book
to all his friends and acquaintances.
In quantities of 100 or more, it
costs no more than a greeting card.

Give

THE FAITH WE HAVE NOT KEPT

to all your friends

Thousands of copies have already been
distributed in every part of the U.S.A.
Employers are giving a book to every
employee, ministers are giving copies
to every church family, doctors are
handing them out to patients. People in
all walks of life are giving them to
friends and associates. DO YOUR PART!

QUANTITY PRICES:

1 copy: **$1**   10 copies: **$5.50**   100 copies: **$35**
25 copies: **$11.50**   500 copies: **$165**
1000 or more copies: **$.30** ea.

(Convenient order form on back of this page)

FOR ADDITIONAL COPIES USE THIS CONVENIENT

ORDER FORM

SEE OTHER SIDE FOR QUANTITY PRICES

THE FAITH WE HAVE NOT KEPT

VIEWPOINT BOOKS
P.O. BOX 9622
SAN DIEGO, CALIF. 92109

Please send me _____ copies of the "THE FAITH WE HAVE NOT KEPT".

Payment of $ _____ is enclosed (send check or money order).

NAME _____

ADDRESS _____

CITY _____ STATE _____ ZIP _____

California residents please add 5% sales tax.

For rush orders shipped Special Handling, add $1 per 100 books or fraction thereof.